How to Make Money Trading Stocks & Commodities

George R. Sranko

toExcel
San Jose New York Lincoln Shanghai

How to Make Money Trading Stocks and Commodities

All Rights Reserved. Copyright © 1990, 1999 by George R. Sranko

No part of this book may be reproduced or transmitted in any form or by any means, graphic, electronic, or mechanical, including photocopying, recording, taping, or by any information storage or retrieval system, without the permission in writing from the publisher.

This edition published by toExcel Press,
an imprint of iUniverse.com, Inc.

For information address:
iUniverse.com, Inc.
620 North 48th Street
Suite 201
Lincoln, NE 68504-3467
www.iuniverse.com

Commodity charts used in this book have been reproduced courtesy of Graphix Commodity Charts. Stock charts used in this book have been reproduced courtesy of Independent Survey Company, Vancouver, B.C. Canada. Copyright 1987 by George R. Sranko.

ISBN: 1-58348-555-4

This book is dedicated to two special people sharing my journey through life; my wife, Jan, and my son, Ryan. They challenge me to do my best every step of the way.

With fun and excitement...

CONTENTS

Preface

Introduction

CHAPTER 1   1
The Big Picture
- Potential for Growth
- Limit Risk
- Have a Timeframe
- Strategy for Success
- Financial Independence

CHAPTER 2   17
Why Make Money?
- Goals
- Visualization
- Narrow the Target
- The 80/20 Rule

CHAPTER 3   23
Master the Line
- A Trading Strategy
- Price Charts
- Trendlines
- Price Level vs Movement Trading
- Technical vs Fundamental
- Price Patterns

CHAPTER 4   47
Trade Patterns Successfully
- Supply and Demand
- Tradeable Patterns
- Established Range
- The Breakout Strategy
- Surging Markets
- Sequential Waves Strategy
- Timing, Timing, Timing

CHAPTER 5   73
Intelligent Trading Tactics
* Predict Direction and Price
* Rules of Trading
* Automatic Entry
* Resting Orders
* Staging In orders
* The Stop Loss
* Reversal Points
* Trailing Stop Loss
* Maximizing Profit

CHAPTER 6   97
Trading Stocks
* Overwhelming Choice
* Stock Charts
* Strategy for Trading Stocks

CHAPTER 7   103
Trading Commodities
* Leverage
* Change in Value
* Longs and Shorts
* Basis
* Seasonal Indicators
* Limit Moves

CHAPTER 8   115
Market Opportunities
* A Line is a Line...
* Trading Currencies
* Precious Metals
* Mutual Funds

Appendix
    Programmed Learning Charts

Biblography

Glossary

Index

Preface

As we enter the third Millennium, there are more and more exciting opportunities for investment. The internet is drastically changing the marketplace and opening a whole new world of possibilities for each of us. Technology in the coming decades will no doubt provide us with tools that we can hardly even imagine today.

At the same time there are ominous signs that cannot be ignored. Humanity is without a doubt dramatically stressing the very life-support systems that all life - including ours -- relies on. We need to remember the basics; clean water, clean air and clean soil. Without a healthy environment we could be super-rich but we would be living the lives of paupers! Imagine a world where you can't breathe without inhaling noxious fumes, can't drink without tasting chemical additives... The true measure of wealth is in our relationships, our quality of life and the quality of our environment.

The techniques I provide in this book work and they work well. By using the approach set out here you can dramatically increase the profit potential of every investment you make. However, like all tools, these must be used wisely.

I challenge you to take aim with your money! Use your investments to support companies, commodities and products that are beneficial to society and to the environment. Before you decide to invest money in a tobacco manufacturer consider how many teenagers who become hooked today will die premature deaths because of lung cancer. Before you invest in a pesticide manufacturer or distributor of genetically modified foods or seeds, consider the cancer-causing agents and genetic disasters-in-the-making being spread throughout our precious air, water and soil.

Use the tools I've provided in this book wisely, for the health of all and for the continued abundance of our home, our planet -- earth. Don't invest in harmful chemicals, deadly armaments, sweat shops using child labor (modern day slavery) - decide to make a positive difference instead! Point your capital in the direction of a positive future for all.

May the coming Millennium bring you and your family much joy and abundance.

Sincerely,

George Sranko

Victoria, B.C.

http://by-George.net/Abundance/

For more info e-mail: abundance@by-george.net

INTRODUCTION

The book in your hand is unlike any other book I have read on the subject of investing or trading the markets for profit.

It is written for the intelligent investor who wants to make a reasonable second income through actively investing in stocks and/or commodities. It is for the person who is not satisfied with someone else calling all the shots or waiting for passive investments to go somewhere.

What I have presented here is a sensible approach to trading based on the experience I have gained over years of active trading. If you are an **inexperienced investor** who would like to trade stocks and commodities but have no idea of where to begin, read on! You will find much of this material just what you are looking for.

Using the approach outlined here you will be able to select stocks or commodities with good profit potential quickly and accurately. You will learn how to trade them from the day you buy until the day you sell (or vice versa). You will learn how to prevent unacceptable losses and turn potential gains into real profits. You will learn automatic entry and exit techniques used primarily by professional traders.

My system is also for the **experienced trader** who wants to maximize profits and perhaps make up for previous losses. It shows you how you can select the best trades without having to wade through years of financial reports and endless newspaper items. It includes detailed information on how you can narrow your research to the few stocks or commodities with the best potential to make money.

I am excited about the material presented in this book. I really believe that this information can change your life by making your trading more rewarding. It has changed mine. With the trading and account management techniques presented here you can realistically expect to make a meaningful amount of money within the next few years.

I don't think of myself as an investor. Investing in the traditional sense is similar to buying a lottery ticket. Very often there is no plan, no strategy, no discipline. If you win it is most often simply a matter of luck. I am more interested in making my own trading decisions based on skill and knowledge; and living with the results.

I consider myself a business manager - the manager of my own trading account. I put my capital to work for the best possible returns. My objective is not 6% or 7% (less after inflation); it is to provide a meaningful source of income to live the lifestyle I choose. I am willing to work towards that end by learning and applying strategies that have proven successful in the past.

I have found that the stock and commodity markets consistently provide returns of 100% to 500% (even 1000%) on the original investment. Level of risk is managed along with all other aspects of my account. The exact amount of money at risk is pre-calculated and trades are entered only if a loss would not jeopardize more than 20% of the account.

The approach I use provides more than simple rules for buying and selling; it is a complete system for managing your own account in a business-like manner. **Perhaps for the first time in your investing career**

As I gained experience I came to realize that winning boils down to one thing; the **correct perspective**. The right attitude is the determining factor in successful trading, or any other pursuit.

There are always positions to take, stocks and commodities to trade, bull markets to get in on... your job is not to trade them all but to trade **only the ones that give you the best opportunities for making money.** Based on your goals and investment criteria - not those of your broker, or your best friend, or a newspaper columnist.

Let the market point the way by learning to trade based on what the market is actually doing, not on what you wish it was doing.

How do you identify a good market to trade?

How do you determine the best time to get in and get out?

Answer these two simple questions successfully for the majority of your trades and you will come out a winner.

Let me show you how in this book.

Chapter 1

The Big Picture

Investment Criteria

The goal of this book is to introduce a reasonable strategy for anyone, almost anywhere, with a couple of thousand dollars or more to invest to make a meaningful amount of money on the stock and commodity markets. Not 6%, 7%, or 8% return but 100%, 200%, 500% or even 1000%!

Without an overwhelming investment of time or training, and with a reasonable, manageable level of risk.

We don't want to merely save what we already have; we want to make it **grow** so that our investment yields a reasonable source of income to allow us to pursue personal goals and dreams. The strategy is based on caution and getting to know one's self as much as on trading techniques and world economic conditions.

There are several important criteria for any investment we are considering to finance our goals. They may vary slightly from person to person but I believe the following requirements are particularly important.

Chapter 1

1. Potential for Growth

If the capital that we presently have at our disposal for investment purposes is to provide a meaningful second income it must grow appreciably year after year.

Growth can be achieved in two primary ways:

    A. By making a **great deal** of money on a **small number** of items, or

    B. By making a **small amount** per unit on a **large number** of items.

Let's say...

Alfred buys a painting worth $10,000 as an investment. He feels that there is a demand for this style of painting entitled "Lion Attacking a Stallion", and that it will appreciate in value over the next few years.

Bob, on the other hand, feels that a series of less expensive prints has a better chance of making a good return than one single painting. He buys 100 different prints for $100 each for a total value of $10,000.

Works of art do moderately well over the next couple of years increasing in value at an average of 10% per year. After two years Alfred may have made 20% or $2,000 on his investment. But what if the market for "Lion Attacking Stallion" type paintings is not as good as he thought and his one painting has only increased 10% over the two year period?

Alfred's return in that case is only $1,000 and he must make a decision. He can hang on to the painting hoping that the market for this style of art picks up or he can sell it and try to make a better investment the next time.

If the average return is 10% per annum Bob will almost certainly come close to that return averaged over his 100 separate

The Big Picture

prints. Some may do poorly and some may do better but the average over two years should yield very close to 20% or $2,000.

Bob can liquidate the $100 prints that don't perform well much more easily than Alfred can his single $10,000 painting. Over several years Bob will have a portfolio of proven performers while Alfred could still be hunting around for the one painting that will make him rich.

I would place my bets on Bob's success at pulling in the higher return over a 5 year period. The **potential for growth** is much better in the real world for a large number of smaller items. Each one makes you only a little bit of money but the total, over the long run, amounts to a lot.

Diversification averages individual losses and gains and diminishes the importance of each single trade.

Make a little bit of money on each item but have hundreds or thousands of those items available to buy or sell as you want to. This is what stocks and commodities allow you to do.

2. Leverage

We all know the principle of using leverage to accomplish more work with less apparent effort. How does this apply to our goal of making money on the markets? The principle of leverage is not confined to teeter-totters or tire irons. Some people are continuously applying financial leverage to accomplish more with the same resources, or even fewer, than that available to many others. They are not all geniuses, magicians, or crooks (although some may be); they are people who have successfully learned to apply leverage.

The most common and universal application of financial leverage is probably used by most of us without even realizing it. The power of borrowing allows us to buy a home or car with little of our own money down and to use that article while we are still paying for it.

Chapter 1

The mortgage on your house is an instrument of financial leverage. Many books have been written about taking advantage of such leverage by using a relatively small amount of your own money to gain control of a piece of real estate which you could otherwise not afford. If a $100,000 property appreciates at 10% a year and you have only $20,000 of your own dollars invested the return on you investment is not 10% but rather 50%.

With stocks and commodities the use of leverage is referred to as buying or selling on margin. Commodities are automatically traded on margin with an actual cash outlay of only 5% to 10% of the contract's value. This is why I see commodities as being particularly important in a program of creating wealth. Trading stocks on margin is more difficult, but certainly possible, and should be discussed with your broker. It is not necessary that you buy stocks on margin; even without leverage it is relatively easy to double or triple your investment in this market.

3. Limited Risk

Everything we do involves a degree of risk. Some say that the **real risk is found in not living your life the way you would like to because of the fear of failure.** I believe that risk is an attitude. Armed with the proper information and experience we can choose our own futures by accepting a certain degree of risk and grabbing life with both hands. Since driving to work in the morning is a risk, why not take a risk in areas where the rewards can make a very real difference to your style of life.

Most people react to the suggestion that they could make money trading commodities with a gasp and an exclamation some- thing like, "Are you crazy? I've heard it's much too risky. You could lose your shirt trading pork bellies!". If these people would take the time to consider the real risks involved and learn how to minimize them they would probably see the market from a different angle.

I am certainly not saying that **everyone** should be actively trading the markets. It just doesn't interest some people. But if you **are** interested don't let the perceptions and unfounded beliefs of the inexperienced get in your way.

The Big Picture

Through knowledge and practical experience we seek to limit our risk. If the risk involved is within certain acceptable limits then we may assume that the venture is reasonably safe to pursue.

Level of risk is also relative to the importance of a venture and the potential rewards. We would all be willing to assume more risk for potentially greater rewards.

Luck is **not** involved in calculating the measure of risk. "Luck is the result of preparation meeting opportunity", as M. LeBoeuf has stated in his book <u>Imagineering</u>. If you need luck to lessen the risk you shouldn't be involved in the first place. Don't jump into a pond full of alligators if your life depends on **the hope** that they won't notice the ripples!

If the risk is within acceptable limits, of course, you would be foolish not to go after rewards which meet your goals and aspirations.

Risk is tempered by knowledge and experience. After all, would any of us have taken our first tentative steps, or gone on that first date, or bought our first used car without willingly accepting some degree of risk?

4. Timeframe

We have all seen those cards in the bank, hanging from the ceiling on long strings, which read something like, "Invest $25 monthly in our Golden Egg Daily Interest Savings Account and within 50 years you can be a MILLIONAIRE!" And probably a rooting medium for daisies as well.

Who wants to wait fifty years to pursue their dreams? I don't think anyone would. If I have to wait that long someone would probably have to come knocking with a long-handled shovel to let me know I had finally made it!

We would all like to make enough money to pursue our dreams while we are still in good enough shape to achieve them, not in fifty years. A reasonable timeframe is required; not a get-

Chapter 1

rich-in-15-days scheme but a plan which aims at giving us a meaningful return on our investment this year, next year, and the year after for as long as we remain interested. And the potential for even more, to become wealthy if we really work at it.

Most of us have jobs and cannot afford to suddenly drop everything to take up treasure hunting full time. Our commitments go on day after day and we have only an hour or two a day (with luck) to spare for learning and applying a strategy. We need a plan that allows us to profit with a minimum of time requirements or commitments.

Plan or Gamble

Before you set out to drive across the city to visit a friend you prepare yourself by taking certain steps to ensure your ability to arrive safely. First of all, and probably most importantly, you learn how to drive. Of course, how ridiculous, you say - everyone knows that!

Not everyone knows it when it comes to investing or trading stocks and commodities! Jumping into the markets without educating yourself and practicing on paper is the same as jumping into a car for the first time and setting out to drive across town. Most people wouldn't think of such foolishness, it would be tantamount to suicide - yet what do they turn around and do with their money? They throw it at some stock because a friend told them it was a good deal, a broker recommended it, or they read about it in the newspaper.

These recommendations **can**, and should, be reasons for considering an investment but they must **remain only a part of your overall strategy and decision to invest or not.**

Otherwise what you are doing is mere gambling - not managing your account for the highest return.

There has to be a system in place that will allow you to take these opinions and recommendations, combine them with your conclusions and put them in proper perspective for decision making.

The Big Picture

The plan should allow us the flexibility of putting into it only as much time and money as we can afford and to give us time off whenever we need it. And it must work without requiring attention every hour or even every day.

Difficult criteria to meet, aren't they? How can anyone make money on the markets with a plan that takes all of this into consideration?

No Hoopla

The secret, in my mind, and the basis of my trading strategy is to keep it simple - no big "Hoopla". I do not mean being ineffective or naive; I mean being smart, and disciplined. An intelligent investor above all. Many investment strategies are based on so-called 'secret formulas'; complex computer programs, automatic indicators, algebraic trend analyzers, and maximum strength ratios (if there is such a thing).

The **market** is the only thing that really counts in this game. What is the market doing, what has it done in the past, and where is it headed? Remember, that is all we have to try and determine. Where is it headed? Instead of guessing, wait for the market to show you and **then** get in.

Success Strategy

Here is the essence of my successful strategy for trading the markets and **making money**.

1. Watch stock and commodity charts for **technical patterns** which can be successfully traded. **Discard** at least 90-95% of potential trades based on their **past price history**. Look for **quiet markets** going sideways, trending up, or trending down.

2. Predict the direction the price will move based on factors such as business fundamentals, company reports, seasonal tendencies, long term trend, past history, 10 year record of prices, trading volume, basis, technical and fundamental considerations. Enter the trade if these factors indicate a move with the trend.

7

Chapter 1

3. Catch the beginning of a move by buying, or selling, as the price breaks out of a quiet, sideways pattern or past a previous point of support or resistance in a trending market. Use the resting order strategy explained later in this book in order to enter at the right time.

4. Once the market makes a move ride with it. Use a **trailing stop loss**, a technique which I will explain in detail in a later chapter, to **lock in a large percentage of the profits.**

   If indicators point to a major move and everything is in your favour add to your position as it breaks the crest of each sequential wave or passes psychological barriers (even increments on the chart, such as 10 cents, 5.00 dollars, etc., depending on the market).

5. Position the stop loss using guidelines described in this book. Use trend lines and reversal points to indicate favorable locations.

6. When the market makes a reversal out of the established trend let the **trailing stop take you out**.

7. Finally, don't try to catch every advance and retreat; that will only kill you (and also age you more quickly, which is even worse).

   Trade for the big moves.

The Big Picture

My very first experience with the markets is a tale that will probably sound familiar to many of you. I once thought that ownership of stocks was limited to sophisticated investors and merely owning shares in a company would automatically put me in that same league! After all, once you had a stock the rest was easy; all you had to do was just hang on until it made money.

The Big Picture

A friend at work had accurate information from a relative who suggested that the shares of a company on the Vancouver stock exchange was due to go up to $5.00 from it's current level of 85 cents in a matter of months. A deal was in the wind with a British company to set up a factory near Vancouver as soon as a few last minute details were worked out.

This was information from a well-informed source, how could I go wrong? I couldn't lose. An inside edge! A chance of a life time! So I phoned up a brokerage firm in Vancouver, opened an account, and purchased my first shares. I also picked up some warrants because the broker recommended them and I didn't know what they were. (They turn out to be an option to buy additional shares within a specified period of time.) I bought them because I didn't want to appear unsophisticated!

The stock bobbed up and down a bit for the next few months but never really did too much, until... until the time arrived for the warrants to be exercised and **then** things really picked up! Everyone with shares was feeling great. The stock was climbing and money was in the air! I picked up another 300 shares with my warrants that day and waited for my fortune to come rolling in.

I waited and waited. That auspicious day, it turned out, marked the peak for "My Great Deal" stock. Right after they had taken my money and shaken me upside down the market fell away. And continued to fall to $2.00, $1.50, $1.00, 50 cents, and lower still to around 20 cents. My profit was gone. My original investment was gone.

I hung on, though, because they were still talking about THE DEAL and it was just a matter of time before my stock would turn around. It had to turn around because that's the way everyone makes money on the stock market! (isn't it?).

After a couple more years of waiting for my Great Deal to materialize I finally sold my shares for 15 cents each. My original $1500 was worth a grand total of $57.50 after about three years. I don't think I'll even bother calculating the monetary return on that investment. Thankfully the knowledge I gained is another story.

Chapter 1

Sound familiar? Some people did make money, but not me. They had a money management system. I had a hot tip, that's all.

What I didn't have was:

1. A game plan,
2. some experience,
3. a mechanism to determine when to get in or out,
4. a system of preserving paper profits (if any),
5. some idea of the past history of this stock,
6. and some fundamentals such as the company's assets, trading volume, and return on invested capital.

What had "Great Deal" been doing before I got involved? Had it ever been as high as the day that I exercised those warrants? Which way was the market headed when I bought? I didn't have a clue.

Have a System

Too many investors find themselves in the same boat - they react to advice of one kind or another, follow up on "Hot Tips", without looking at the Big Picture and judging for themselves. How many people do you know who approach the markets in exactly the same way that I describe above?

If I **learn** how to trade the markets I have a life skill which will carry me through times of inflation, depression, and all the highs and lows in between. I will learn how to deal with the ups and downs in life and how to come out a winner in the long run. If I depended solely on someone else trading for me I wouldn't learn anything about the skills required to make it in the market place or anywhere else.

In my trading I decide where my money goes based on a plan, past experience, as well as outside advice. Why? Because I am more interested in my account than any one else. It is my hard earned cash and I am prepared to wait patiently for just the right move. I don't have to trade every day to make someone else think

The Big Picture

I am on the ball. Overtrading leads mainly to one thing - high commissions.

If you agree with what I am saying and plan on following the strategy outlined in this book you will **avoid managed accounts**. By a managed account I mean giving a broker or anyone else the freedom to trade your account for you; to enter and exit trades when and how they want to.

Ultimately you are the only one interested in nurturing your own account and **ensuring** that it makes money. It may be easier to let someone else make the decisions but, believe me, in the long run you will do **far better on your own** by patiently applying your own system and learning what the markets have to teach.

I am not saying that advice is not to be valued. Advice **should be considered** in your trading strategy but it should only be one of many factors used in your decision to buy or sell.

A friend of mine once became so interested in trading, after attending a short seminar I presented, that he couldn't wait the three or four months I recommend for trading on paper. He phoned a broker to set up an account right away and was talked into a managed account. I did not hear about this until more than a month had passed and by then the broker had lost money. I immediately recommended to my friend that he take his money and manage his own account. I felt he should start slowly and wait patiently for just the right patterns to develop. He decided to hang on for just one more week and lost another thousand dollars. Thankfully he pulled out before all of his money was gone.

The broker had traded his account mercilessly day after day. One day he would buy porkbellies, lose money and get out, only to turn around and sell short the next day. To my way of thinking you plan on profiting from a commodity either as it goes up or as it goes down. A broker is often under a lot of pressure to trade your account daily to show you he is working hard to make you money, and also to make his commissions.

Some of those who manage accounts professionally may feel I am too critical. I am sure you would agree that an investor will do

Chapter 1

better **over the long run** by learning a system that works and developing the self-discipline to stick with it.

If you want to make a lot of money trading on the markets it is almost essential that **you** make the decisions, profit from your successes, and learn from your mistakes. Do this and you have a life-skill; an ability which is depression and inflation proof!

A System for You

In this book I am presenting a system which I know will lead me to financial freedom within the next ten years. How do I know? Intuition is part of it, a feeling of inevitability. Primarily, though, the process I have laid out for myself leads unerringly in that direction. It is based on the power of knowledge, patience, and the limitless potential of stock and commodity trading.

The following steps are the guts of my plan to become financially independent. The rest is experience, learning, and patience. Perseverance and self-discipline help to keep me on track.

How many of us have heard the old saying, "This moment is the beginning of the rest of our lives", but never really believed it? The journey, as we all know, is what really counts; the fact that you tried. If you fall, pick yourself up, dust- off, figure out why you fell, and keep on exploring life. Above all, have fun!

The Journey

Step 1: **Knowledge**

> Learn as much about trading, and the markets you are interested in, as you can get your hands on. Digest this information and try the strategies I recommend in this book. They are the best I know of. Decide on the mechanics of trading which you will adhere to, at least initially, and test them in marketplace (on paper at this stage).

The Big Picture

Write your trading strategy and rules down on paper and refer to them often as you learn. Test new ideas by paper-trading for a few months.

Step 2: **Experience - On Paper**

As you are learning, reading, digesting - you can begin to trade the actual markets on paper. **Get hold of commodity or stock charts immediately.** Take advantage of the introductory offer most chart services make for $10 to $25.

Look at a wide cross-section of commodities or stocks at this stage and be prepared to spend at least half an hour to an hour a day updating the charts that appear promising based on the patterns you are watching for.

Follow the recommendations and system I present in this book and trade as if you had actual cash involved in the market. This means using charts and following the markets, actually marking buy/sell orders and stop losses **on the charts**, and keeping track of fictional profits and losses. All of this is laid out in the following pages. Try it on paper. No cash is involved - but everything else is the same as the real thing.

Do this for a minimum of three or four months. If you are holding your own or have made a profit (on paper) you are ready for the next step. If not, keep on paper trading until you can make money without the pressures and worries of the real thing. Don't kid yourself - the real thing is tougher!

Step 3: **Enter with Cash**

Now you are swimming in deep water! Cash is on the line. The name of this game is not profit - not yet. It is **survival**. For the first year you are going to attempt to survive in the jungle, running with the rest of the pack.

Chapter 1

Commodities:

About 85% of commodity traders lose in the first year. They have no strategy or discipline. By the time you finish reading this book and paper trading for a few months you will **know** if you can become successful in the actual market. It becomes a question of **how** successful.

The potential to profit becomes a very real opportunity with your knowledge and experience at this stage. You know that it can be done and the urge is to trade every minute of every day with wild abandon. Yield to this urge and it will become your undoing. You must exhibit **restraint, perseverance, and self-discipline** if you are to survive the first year of real trading. Be cautious and conservative in your approach.

Stocks:

At this point I would stick to one market - stocks or commodities. The choice depends on which one you are more comfortable with, what your risk threshold is, and what your financial goals are.

With stocks the risks are often less but the potential rewards are proportionately reduced as well. You can still make a great deal of money by using the information in this book for trading shares. If stocks are your preference, go for it!

The secret in the first year, once again, is to be cautious and nurture your account rather than throw money around carelessly to see if any of it connects with a winner.

Step 4: **Practice and Patience**

This is the most difficult step. The patience to wait for **just the right markets and moves** and to enter trades **only** when you have a good opportunity to make money.

This is the process of selecting and extracting only markets that meet the criteria you have previously laid out in your system; your business plan.

The Big Picture

The overwhelming tendency at this stage is to want to trade every market and to make a fortune right away. Why wait? By this time you can see the potential and you want to trade every minute to see those profits come rolling in. And this is the biggest mistake you can make.

This is the time for extra caution and continued learning. This is when many potentially good traders become trapped. They become over confident and trade relentlessly trying to speed up what can be a long haul.

At this stage limit yourself to one or two contracts per commodity or under a thousand dollars worth of stocks. **Do this for one to two years after you start trading with cash.** You will be making money and learning at the same time. And don't become frustrated with starting small and building slowly, patiently. You are preparing the foundations for the next step.

Step 5.   **Create Wealth**

This is the final stage. You will be a seasoned trader, a professional, if you have the discipline and patience to go this far. You will be ready for the ultimate game in town; wealth creation.

Using information presented in this book, particularly the breakout, sequential waves and scaling-in strategies. you will use the market's own momentum to build wealth. At this point you will start to scale-in orders for 5, 10 or even more contracts per commodity or thousands of shares on the stock markets.

It will be only a matter of time before you get in on a big move that will make you thousands, or even tens of thousands, of dollars.

Some of you will make a moderate amount of money, some will make a fortune, and others will become wealthy. Here is the most startling fact of all - **it is completely up to you**! You have the information right here in your hand; provide the will, the goals, the desire and **you will accomplish whatever you set out to do.**

How far do **you** want to go?

15

Chapter 1

Summary

1. In order to make money on the markets your strategy must include good potential for growth, the means to limit risk, and a reasonable time frame.

2. Prepare for success through education and experience. Have a written strategy which you can follow like a road map.

3. Have the patience to practice this strategy and stick to it. Refine and improve it as you go along but know when to stop. When your system is working the money will seem to flow into your account and you will know that you deserve it.

Chapter 2

Why Make Money?

Goals

The first step in finding a solution to any problem is to decide on what you want. What is your goal? What specifically are you looking for?

Too many people generalize by saying they want a "better life" or "a long holiday" or "lots of money". This sounds fine but the human mind deals in pictures. Think of a bright red barn with a cow standing beside the door. What color is the cow? Is it brown, black and white, cream?

You will know what color it is because, as soon as I mentioned the red barn, you saw the scene just as I described it. Each person reading this sentence will have a different picture based on past experiences, interests, etc., etc.

Think of the phrase "lots of money" and let your mind paint a picture of what this means to you. Your mind needs something concrete to work with; an image to concentrate on.

Define and clarify exactly what you want so that you can:

1. picture it in your mind's eye, and

2. make it attainable within a reasonable time frame.

Chapter 2

These are two powerful techniques used by **super achievers** in order to attain goals which might seem impossible to the average person.

Visualization

The human mind deals most effectively with problems and solutions in terms of pictures or mental images. You must have a detailed and comprehensive goal in order to be able to translate it into a picture. Generalities such as "making lots of money" or "having a good time" are the result of wishes and hopes but do not offer solutions. Visualization flexes the mind and allows you the opportunity to mentally picture and experience success in a way that matters most to you as an individual.

Scientists have shown that repeated visualization of an activity or goal yields almost as many positive benefits as the actual experience would. The subconscious mind cannot differentiate between what is imagined and what is real. If you picture yourself in the situation you would most like to experience the mind stores this information just as if it had really happened. The more "real" or palpable you can make this image the more effective this mental practice will be.

Is it your goal to make lots of money? It probably is but this is not specific enough. How much would you need, for example, to pay off your mortgage? Or to put down for that new house? Or to buy that shiny red Mercedes sport coupe?

Once you determine **what** your first step will be when you have money it becomes a concrete goal. There is a dollar value and there is an image in your mind of the house, the car, the holiday... or whatever it may be.

You can picture yourself paying off the mortgage on your house, for example. Go through the whole process - taking the money to the bank and depositing it, holding the discharge papers in your hand, tearing the mortgage document in two (feel the paper resist and the sound of tearing as it finally yields), and feeling the sense of satisfaction this will bring you.

Why Make Money?

Go through the same process for your own goal - the new house or the car - visualizing each step from the time you write the cheque to the feeling you will have sitting in the living room looking out over the ocean or behind the wheel zooming down that twisting road in the mountains.

Try to experience the sensations, sounds, sights and emotions just as if you were involved in doing the real thing. And someday you will.

Do this for 15 minutes every day, or more often if you wish, and it becomes just a matter of time.

Narrow the Target

The second important technique used by super-achievers is the fragmentation of one big problem into many smaller ones. If your goal is to "become a millionaire by the age of 40" and you have nothing but holes in your pockets you will probably be so overwhelmed by the sheer immensity of the task that you give up and go back to sleep instead. But take that same goal and make it something attainable by thinking of the first step, aiming for it, accomplishing it and then moving on to the next step.

Your first step may be to get your pockets sewn up. Your next might be to save up enough money for this book or a notebook to fill with your accomplishments. You are on your way - bit by manageable bit. The immediate goal is no longer the tallest peak in the range; it is one ridge, then the next, then the next peak, on and on... until one day the final summit stands shining before your eyes.

If it is difficult to imagine what your first step should be and how it ties into the larger picture, try working backwards from the goal. Starting with the goal in mind ask yourself "Could I achieve this tomorrow?". If not, ask yourself what you would have to do first. Could you accomplish it tomorrow? If not what would you have to do before that step? In this fashion you will come to a step that **can** be achieved tomorrow - your first step!

Chapter 2

Deadlines

Use time as an aid in defining your goals, not as a hindrance. Give yourself 10 years to make a million dollars and there is no immediacy to your goal. There is no reason to do anything this minute or even tomorrow because you always have years in which to get down to business. But if one of the first steps on your road to riches is defined as "making $10,000 in the first six months (by such and such a date)" you have a reasonable target within a workable timeframe. And you better get going on it right now because you don't have any time to waste!

Motivation

Success breeds success. We have all heard it before. But do you feel it in your bones?

Specific goals can guide your energies and give your life a focus. They motivate you to keep plugging away in a direction that **you** set for yourself.

If you have the interest, the determination, the time and a plan you can achieve anything.

Priorities

Define your goals in writing and priorize them. Spend the majority of your time on the most important goals. There is a rule, the 80/20 Rule, which states that in a large number of items 80% of the value of the total will be found in approximately 20% of the items.

Achieve 20% of your goals, the most important ones, and 80% of your aims will be satisfied.

Summary

1. Use **visualization** to paint a graphic, detailed mental picture of your goal. Try to experience the success of reaching this goal by playing a movie in your mind, complete with sound and sensation, of yourself doing what you would most like to do.

2. **Divide your goal** into bite-size, manageable pieces and think of each of them as a milestone along the way. Focus on the immediate, short-term goal and **enjoy the journey**. Do not become so goal oriented that the journey means nothing and, when you finally do arrive, there is no satisfaction. Take the time to enjoy each experience because really that is the **ultimate goal**, isn't it?

3. Give yourself a realistic **time frame** for achieving your goals. If there is no time frame you are just dreaming.

4. Use the **80/20 Rule** to priorize your tasks and remember that you will accomplish 80% of what you are after by concentrating on the 20% that is the most important. We usually do just the opposite.

Chapter 3

Master the Line

A Trading Strategy

The Line

If you could determine the future you would have the means to become wealthy beyond all the dreams that you presently nurture. But... what if you can only guess at the future and yet learn how to benefit if patterns and occurrences develop in the manner you had predicted? And also learn how to get out without losing everything if you turn out to be wrong!

Learn techniques and strategies which allow you to do this and you could still become wealthy even though you **cannot know** what the future holds. You can do it because **you can make a lot when you are right and only lose a little when you are wrong**. In the end profit will prevail over losses. Do this enough times and eventually you will have more than enough money to pursue your goals.

Graph any series of past events over time and you get a line wandering across the page. Someone once said that "history repeats itself" and we all know this to be true. A line in the future will be just like a line from the past with all of it's potentials and probabilities. If we practice understanding price histories from the past we have a better understanding of how they may behave in the future.

Chapter 3

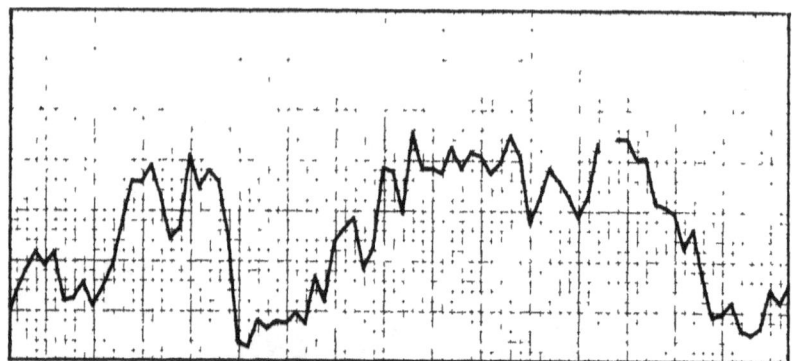

Figure 3-1. *This line could be a representation of the change in your brain function during a night's sleep, a record of your driving time to work over the last month, the price of Orange Juice for the last six months on the New York exchange, or the price of IBM shares for the last year. It doesn't really matter.*

A line is a line, is a line - learn how to follow and profit from it with the right frame of mind, without losing your initial capital, and **you can eventually build wealth starting with very little!**

Price Charts

The price range and change in value of any item of trade can be graphed over time to give you a picture of both historical and current prices. If you had your home appraised once every month over a 5 year period, for example, you would have the raw data for a graph which would be an accurate record of housing price trends in your neighborhood for that time period. Depending upon the state of the real estate market the price line may go up and down in a narrow range, steadily up over the years, or maybe even steadily down.

When market prices are graphed over a period of time you end up with a line which looks like any other. A typical price chart would look like the following graph.

Master the Line

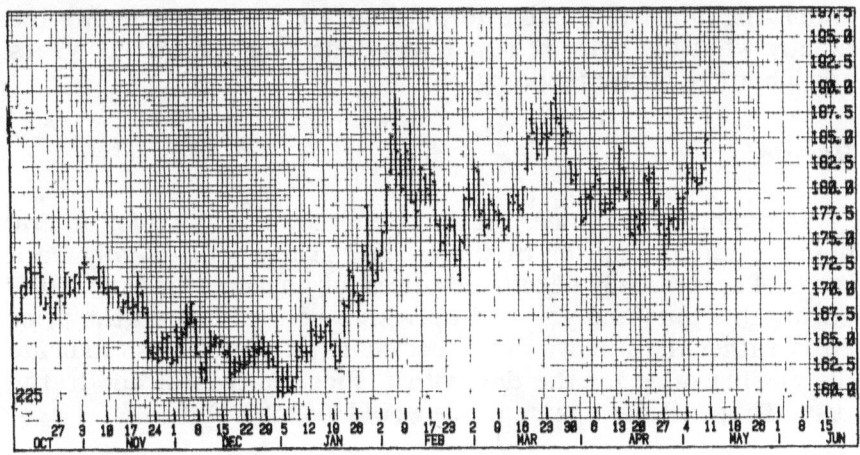

Figure 3-2. *Price chart. This chart indicates the change in value of an item over a period of time. The horizontal axis of a price chart carries the exact dates involved and the vertical axis has a scale of relevant prices.*

Importance of Charts

Price charts are used much more extensively in trading commodities than stocks, although stock charts are available **and should be used!** Why all serious stock traders do not follow them I cannot fathom.

A chart showing an accurate history of any stock or commodity is invaluable in making the **most important** decision of all; **which ones to avoid!** That's right. **Discarding the vast majority of markets and selecting the few that have the potential to make you money is the most important first step in making a successful trade**. Charts make the selection of potentially rewarding trades much quicker and more accurate than any other technique that I know of.

Chapter 3

If I am considering a trade in sugar, for example, it is important to me to be able to pull out a chart which shows me exactly what the price of sugar has done over the last 10 years and what it is currently doing.

Range

Bargaining over prices on the open market goes on for several hours each trading, or business, day. There will usually be a range of successfully negotiated prices for any stock or commodity during this time and you end up with a vertical line on the price chart rather than just a dot. Most chart publishers also indicate the closing price for the day with a short horizontal line to the right. Thus one day's price range would look like this:

7.00   ├

6.00

In a newspaper this range would appear as the following quote:

	Hi	Lo	Close
Oct. Sugar	7.20	6.72	7.00

FINANCIAL FUTURES

```
—Contract—                                    Open
High  Low              High  Low Settle Chg   Int
```

CANADIAN DOLLAR (IMM)
100,000 dollars; $(U.S.) per Canadian dollar

High	Low		High	Low	Settle	Chg	Open Int
.7543	.6770	Mar	.7467	.7424	.7466	+57	15,659
.7525	.6995	Jun	.7447	.7398	.7446	+58	5,923
.7819	.6950	Sep	.7400	.7372	.7426	+59	1,786
.7504	.6960	Dec	.7400	.7369	.7406	+60	630
.7496	.7052	Mar			.7386	+61	95

Last spot .7468, up 47.
Est. sales 4,111. Thu.'s sales 5,607.
Thu.'s open int 24,093, off 139.

BRITISH POUND (IMM)
25,000 pounds; $ per pound

1.5390	1.3680	Mar	1.5240	1.5090	1.5225	+100	24,168
1.5220	1.3550	Jun	1.5090	1.4960	1.5080	+100	1,611
1.5080	1.3420	Sep	1.4880	1.4800	1.4935	+100	366
1.4820	1.3675	Dec	1.4700	1.4700	1.4830	+100	181

Last spot 1.5245, up 90.
Est. sales 3,517. Thu.'s sales 4,746
Thu.'s open int 26,326, off 268.

WEST GERMAN MARK (IMM)
125,000 marks; $ per mark

.5661	.4370	Mar	.5511	.5457	.5508	+23	53,308
.5692	.4850	Jun	.5543	.5492	.5540	+23	4,985
.5725	.4868	Sep	.5530	.5522	.5568	+22	423

Last spot .5491, up 20.
Est. sales 25,056. Thu.'s sales 34,272.
Thu.'s open int 58,773, off 321.

FRENCH FRANC (IMM)
$ per franc; 1 point equals $0.00001

| .16675 | .14500 | Mar | | | .16400 | | 316 |
| | | Jun | | | .16000 | | 2 |

Last spot .16497, up 64.
Thu.'s sales 56.
Thu.'s open int 318, off 47.

SWISS FRANC (IMM)
125,000 francs; $ per franc

.6753	.5125	Mar	.6516	.6458	.6515	+32	32,993
.6800	.5850	Jun	.6565	.6508	.6563	+34	2,660
.6830	.5948	Sep	.6580	.6549	.6603	+33	402
.6860	.5970	Dec			.6643	+18	10

Last spot .6489, up 25.
Est. sales 20,247. Thu.'s sales 26,191.
Thu.'s open int 36,065, up 567.

JAPANESE YEN (IMM)
12.5 million yen; $ per yen

.006670	.005850	Mar	.006527	.006510	.006522	+12	29,179
.006707	.006121	Jun	.006562	.006546	.006560	+12	2,215
.006745	.006160	Sep	.006600	.006583	.006598	+12	103
.006750	.006231	Dec	.006628	.006628	.006637	+12	7

Last spot .006500, off 83.
Est. sales 7,391. Thu.'s sales 11,179.
Thu.'s open int 31,504, off 544.

EURODOLLAR (IMM)
$1 million; points of 100%

94.32	87.64	Mar	93.59	93.50	93.50		97,043
94.15	88.84	Jun	93.62	93.54	93.54	+.03	80,672
94.03	89.29	Sep	93.55	93.55	93.55	+.04	38,994
93.88	90.18	Dec	93.57	93.50	93.50	+.06	24,263
93.67	90.94	Mar	93.45	93.37	93.38	+.08	14,656
93.61	91.69	Jun	93.25	93.16	93.20	+.10	10,441
93.26	91.70	Sep	93.03	92.95	92.99	+.11	9,040
93.07	92.25	Dec	92.81	92.73	92.78	+.12	6,406

Est. sales 96,216. Thu.'s sales 91,616.
Thu.'s open int 281,715, off 1,781.

TREASURY BONDS (CBT)
$100,000; points 32nds of 100%

High	Low		High	Low	Settle	Chg	Open Int
102-30	56-27	Mar	99 26	99 12	99 16	+05	221,424
102 5	63-12	Jun	98-26	98-12	98-16	+04	65,940
101-22	63-4	Sep	97 27	97-15	97 18	+04	8,520
101-10	62-24	Dec	96-28	96-18	96-21	+05	3,589
100-26	67	Mar	96	95-22	95-25	+06	3,151
99-23	66 25	Jun	95 5	94-28	94-30	+06	1,834
99-12	76-58	Sep	94-11	94-2	94-4	+06	2,239
99-2	85-16	Dec			93 11	+06	450
95-10	85-18	Mar			92-19	+06	18
93-27	85-25	Jun			91 29	+06	9
91 16	89 17	Sep			91-9	+06	5

Est. sales 195,000. Thu.'s sales 234,129
Thu.'s open int 307,179, up 3,084.

U.S. TREASURY BILLS (IMM)
$1 million, points of 100%

95.07	89.58	Mar	94 39	94.29	94.32	+.04	27,814
94.97	90.50	Jun	94.45	94.36	94.38	+.04	17,036
94.92	90.83	Sep	94.47	94.39	94.41	+.05	2,369
94.81	91.48	Dec	94.45	94.37	94 38	+.06	1,126
94.63	92.18	Mar	94.33	94.28	94.29	+.07	654
94.40	93.05	Jun	94.18	94 16	94.15	+.08	247
94.18	93.90	Sep			93.97	+.09	58
93.94	93.49	Dec			93.79	+.10	5

Est. sales 10,116. Thu.'s sales 8,241
Thu.'s open int 49,309, up 1

10-YR. TREASURY NOTES (CBT)
$100,000; points 32nds of 100%

105-4	89-15	Mar	104	103 21	103 21	+03	46,324
104-11	98 8	Jun	103 7	102 28	102 28	+02	12,692
103-12	97 15	Sep	102 11	102 2	102 2	+01	56
101-8	96-20	Dec			101 9	+01	

Thu.'s sales 17,915.
Thu.'s open int 59,072, up 639

S&P COMPOSITE (CME)—points and cents

283.40	227.35	Mar	282.30	275.70	282.05	+5.30	102,483
284.90	228.90	Jun	283.60	277.00	283.50	+5.35	12,319
285.95	229.90	Sep	284.20	278.40	284.65	+5.35	246
286.50	243.20	Dec	285.20	279 00	285.75	+5.25	20

Last index 279.70, up 4.08.
Thu.'s sales 88,728.
Thu.'s open int 115,068, up 197.

VALUE LINE (KCBT)—points and cents

260.00	210.00	Mar	259.35	254.50	257 10	+1.60	10,109
258.50	219.50	Jun	258.00	253.00	256.10	+1.95	1,512
257.50	222.00	Sep	253.00	252.50	255.30	+1.90	84
253.50	240.00	Dec	253.00	253.00	254.55	+2.15	10

Last index 260.35, up 2.13.
Thu.'s sales 3,820.
Thu.'s open int 11,715, up 261

NYSE COMPOSITE (NYFE)—points, cents

161.75	128.00	Mar	161.00	157.60	160.80	+2.50	9,424
162.60	131.05	Jun	161.75	158.50	161.60	+2.45	1,953
163.55	133.90	Sep	162.25	159.25	162.40	+2.45	486
164.50	140.30	Dec	163.00	160.00	163.20	+2.45	37

Last index 159.56, up 1.98.
Est. sales 14,135. Thu.'s sales 12,388.
Thu.'s open int 11,900, off 88.

Chapter 3

Price Quotes

In the accompanying example of a newspaper page with futures price quotes you can see that the information is displayed in columns under the headings Contract - High & Low, High, Low, Settle, Change, and Open Interest. The first group, contract highs and lows, refer to the extreme price ranges of the contract since it originally began trading.

The main group refers to the trading activity of the previous day. Take a closer look at the Canadian Dollar quoted above. The March contract traded in a range from a high of .7467 to a low of .7424 and closed at .7466. This close is .0057 higher than the previous day's close. This market has good liquidity because there are 15,659 contracts which are open and remain to be settled. I recommend trading futures contracts with a minimum open interest of 5,000 or so.

Stocks are reported in a similar fashion and show high, low, and close for the previous day's trading. Liquidity is indicated by the number of shares sold each day. It is a good idea to restrict your trading to those stocks with a volume of at least 10 to 20,000 shares traded per day.

Charting

Price charts for markets you are following should be updated each day from the newspaper or over the phone from your brokerage firm. I concentrate on the highs and lows and chart the complete range for each day. Some traders chart only the close or settlement price but I like to know if a stock or commodity has made a large move up and then come back down, or if it was a quiet day with very little movement.

If you are using charts with weekly, instead of daily, ranges keep track of the highs and lows for the week or look at the summary published each Saturday in the financial newspapers. Stock charts are often prepared showing weekly price ranges since securities are not normally as volatile as futures contracts.

When a series of these price ranges are put to paper they snake across the graph to yield a historic price chart for that particular commodity or security. This give you **a line to follow, to learn from and to profit from.**

It doesn't matter so much what commodity or stock the line represents but rather **how it behaves**.

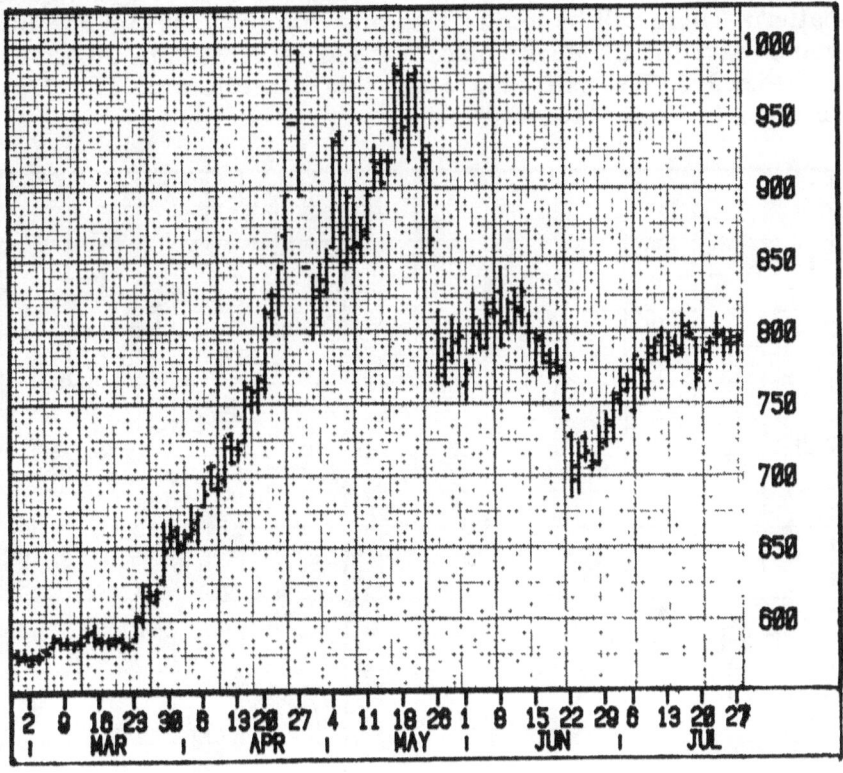

Figure 3-3. A typical daily price chart resulting in a line meandering across the page. Some of the things to look for are volatility or the daily trading range; speed of any change in value; and current price compared to historical price levels.

Chapter 3

Trends

Prices can only go in three directions; up, down, and sideways. Sometimes it is difficult to determine what prices are doing if we are concerned with hourly or even daily movements. But put a long line of past price ranges together and you get a pattern. There will be lots of dips and bumps along the line but you should still be able to discern a general direction - up, down, or sideways. **We can help spot this direction or trend by drawing in lines - "trendlines".**

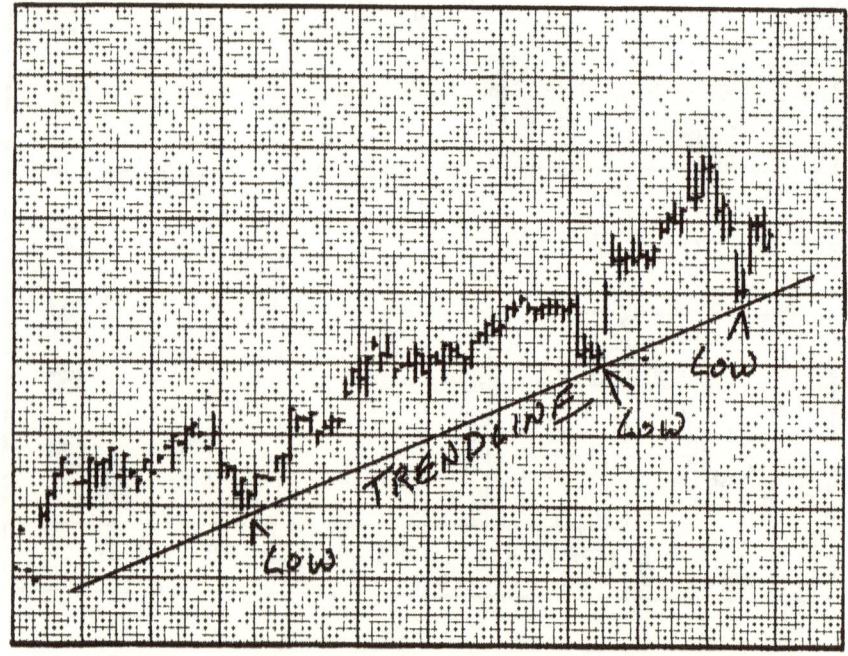

Figure 3-4. Example of an up trend market on a price chart. This trendline has been drawn by connecting as many successive lows as possible. An up trending trendline represents major support for prices as long as it is not violated. Another line connecting highs could also be drawn to indicate the top of the established trend.

Master the Line

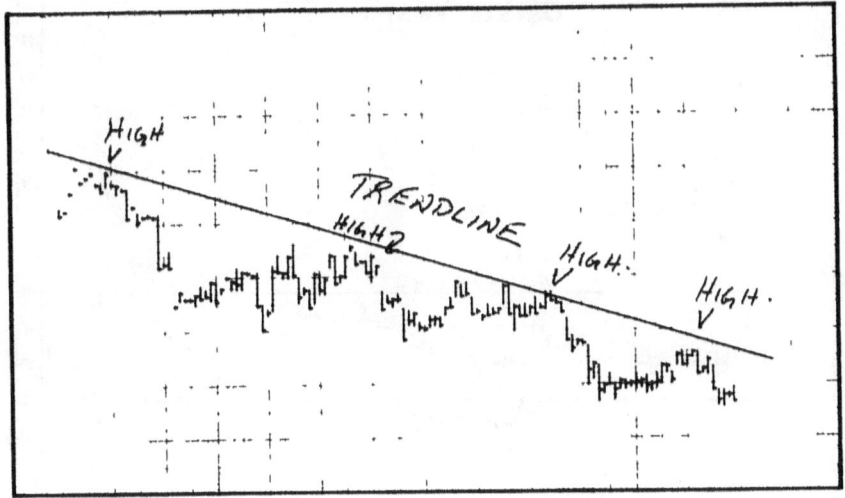

Figure 3-5. Example of a down trend market on a price chart. Down trending trendlines are drawn by connecting the successive highs. This trendline indicates a major line of resistance.

We have seen how trends can push and pull the price up or down. Markets can also enter a period of quiet stability where the price forms a horizontal line sideways across the page. A sideways trend may not form an attractive trade at the moment because the price really isn't going anywhere. But it does offer excellent **potential** for profit.

Chapter 3

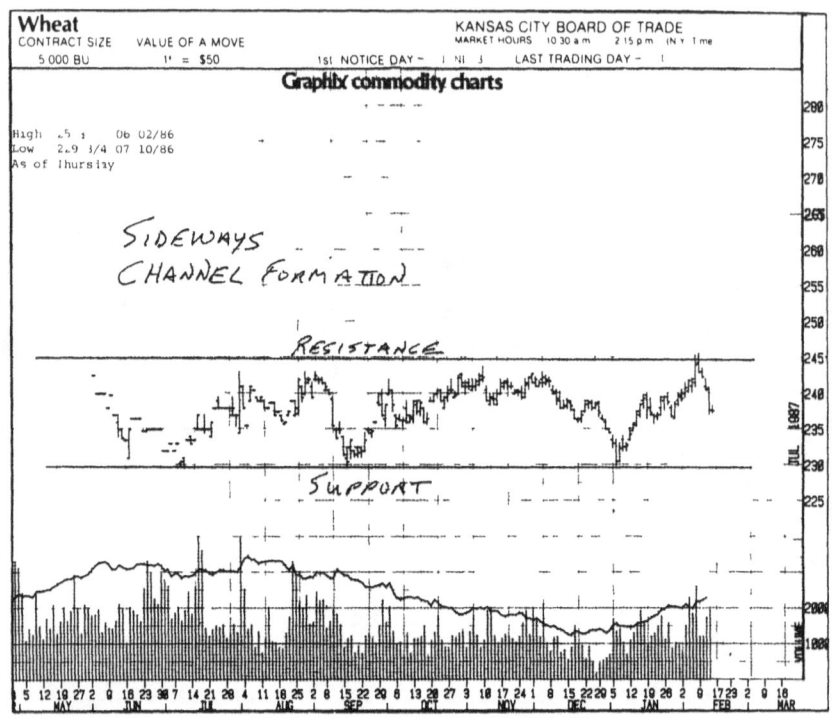

Figure 3-6. *An example of a **sideways channel**. This pattern represents stability between supply and demand in the marketplace. Trendlines for this type of market, also referred to as a congestion phase or a narrow trading range, are drawn by connecting **both** the highs and lows. Prices in this type of market can break upward **or** downward so it is valuable to establish the top and bottom of the range.*

Duration of Trend

In order to make a lot of money on your trades you must look for **big moves**. Get in early and ride them to the limit and you can take in profits day after day for weeks on end based on a plan and the initial decision to play a particular market. Once you are in position the money keeps rolling in with no effort on your part; that is the type of market we are looking for. This is what can take us from the arena of making $10.50 per hour to earning hundreds in an hour!

Master the Line

A. **Short term trend** - this is a trend which is established over a few days. It may be in any direction and has little potential to make us money.

A strong thrust, however, **may** indicate the beginning of a move into new ground. Particularly if it crosses a medium or long term trend line. Think of it as an early warning system; a sign to be prepared for a larger move.

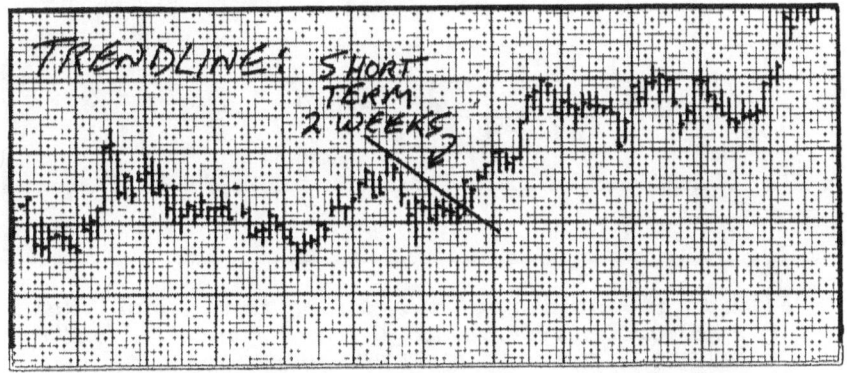

Figure 3-7. Price chart indicating a **short term trend**. The short term trend is always the **current** trend. It may not necessarily be in the same direction as the mid or longterm trend, as in this case.

B. **Medium term trend** - this is a trend that occurs over weeks to 2 or 3 months. All big moves must start with a short term thrust building to a medium term trend. Important to watch.

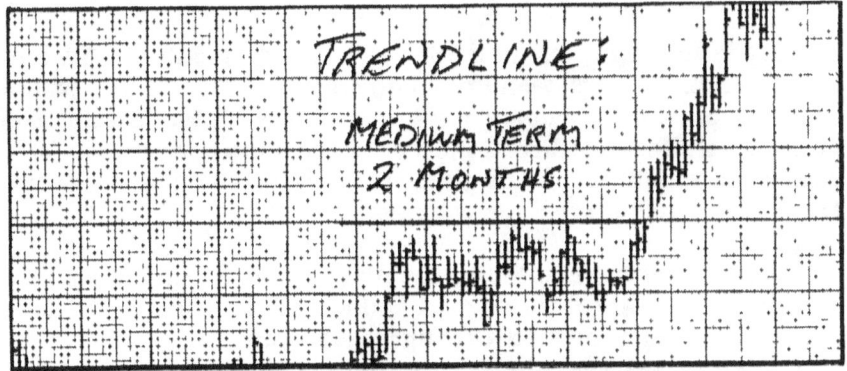

Figure 3-8. An example of a **medium term trend** on the same chart as figure 3-7. A trend is considered to be medium term if it is between one month and three months in length.

Chapter 3

C. **Long term trend** - I consider a trend over three months to be a long term trend. I trade with the long term trend, with few exceptions. You don't try to outwit the market and succeed at making money!

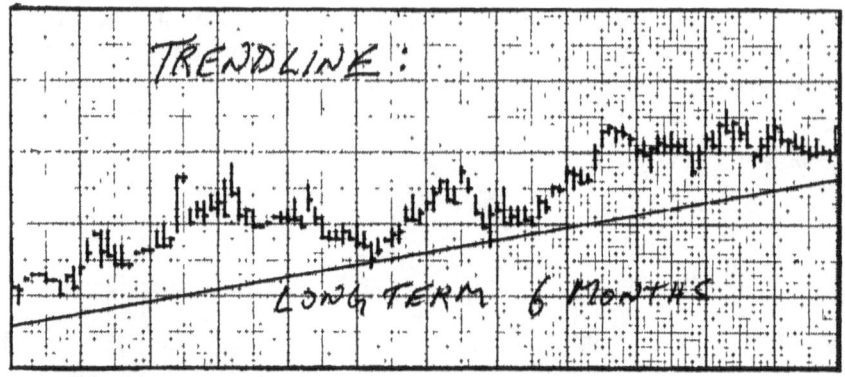

Figure 3-9. An illustration of a **long term trend**. This trend has been established for over 6 months and is still holding. I consider any trend which has continued unbroken for over 3 months to be a long term trend, and of some significance. **This is the trend to trade with** in the majority of cases. It can be thought of as the driving force behind the price and, until a fundamental change occurs in the marketplace, it will continue to do so.

Putting It All Together

In the following example all three (short, medium and long term) trendlines have been drawn on one chart, just as you will be doing. It becomes obvious that you can have all three trendlines going in **different** directions or in the **same** direction. The relationship between them gives us clues or signals concerning the **future** direction the line will take.

The long term trend is up, the medium term trend is also up, but the current short term trend is down. The current short term trend has, in fact, **broken through** the medium term trend. Does this mean that we should phone up our broker and sell immediately? No - but it **is a signal** to watch for either further weakening or a reversal and a re-establishment of the medium term uptrend.

Master the Line

The line has broken through an established range. How long had the range been established? The time scale along the bottom of the chart indicates roughly 3 months. The line has broken out of a range which had been holding for more than three months.

If the market continued to decline and the line broke down through the long term trendline it would be even more significant. Once again, examining the chart, we can see that the long term trend has been established for about eight months. If the line breaks **out** of a range which has held for eight months **we know, without question**, that some fundamental change has occurred in this particular marketplace.

Chapter 3

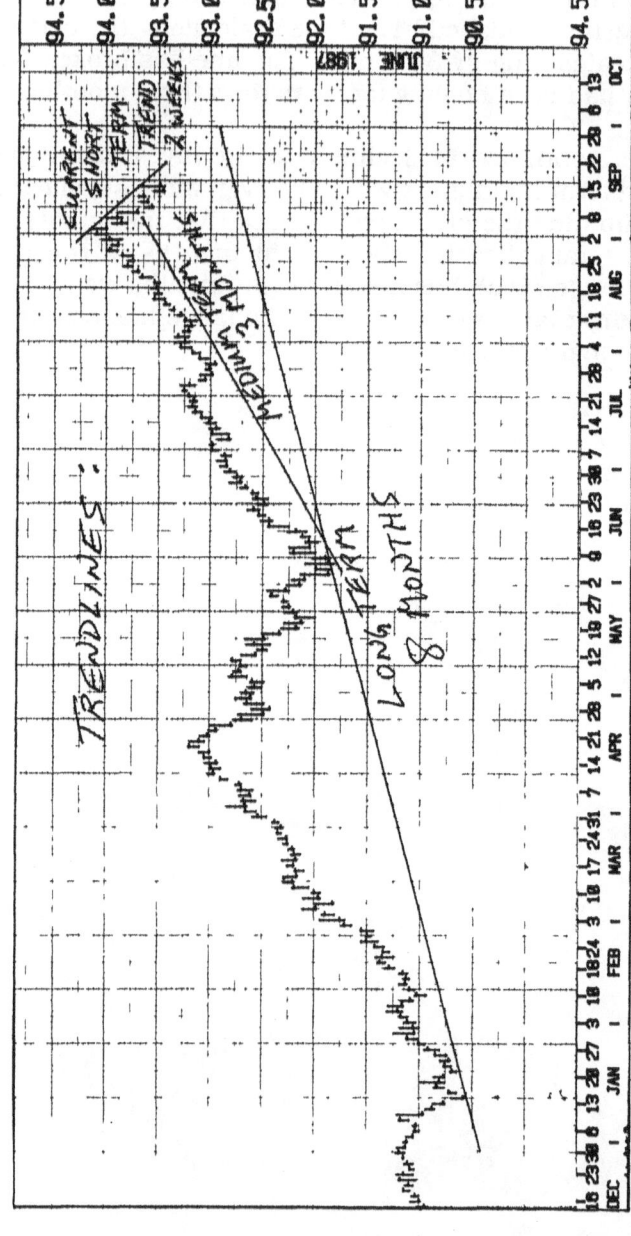

Figure 3-10 *All three trends, short, medium and long term, have been defined on this chart by drawing in lines of support and resistance. The up trend is extremely well established but some day it too will fail. The current short term trend has broken through the medium term line. This is an indicator to watch and wait for further developments. Will the line continue downward to break through the long term support line or will it bounce back?*

What Is... Is

Trendlines and re-occurring patterns are used to give important signals concerning future price movements. They are like the signposts and red flags we encounter every day as we drive from home to the office, or from one end of town to the other.

The line on a chart is a historical price record. There can be no arguing with it, no mystery, no discussion ... it simply is. In the world of markets the price chart is the closest thing there is to a distillation of all the factors influencing the past, present, and future value of a particular stock or commodity.

Study this price chart and as many others as you can get your hands on; learn to work with them and use them as an important tool in your trading strategy. They are the **only thing** you can count on as you go from one market to the next and from one day to the next.

Most of what many traders use in making trading decisions is based on hope, greed, conjecture, rumour, and hhhot tips! Charts instantly bring you back to reality.

Breaking a Trend

In general, unless I have good reason to do otherwise, **I trade with the medium and long term trends**. Any time a medium or long term trend is violated, though, **a fundamental change has occurred in the psychology of that particular marketplace**. This is an important signal alerting me to the potential for further, and likely profitable, developments. I am particularly interested if it is also a **pattern** which I have successfully traded in the past, such as a breakout from a channel.

Chapter 3

What is a Trend?

Give the same chart to ten people and ask them to draw in trend lines and you will probably get at least four or five different lines. Trade for a while and you will develop a feel for trend lines that mean something in terms of areas of support and resistance.

The simplest approach is to draw long term trend lines first and work towards short term lines. Try to connect peaks and troughs which obviously contain the line, almost as a taut electric fence would.

Strength in a Trendline

Two factors indicate the strength of any trend line:

1. The length of the line (indicating time period). The longer the trend the more authority it carries, and

2. The number of times the market has touched the line and bounced off. The more peaks or troughs that touch such a trend line the greater the indicated strength.

Master the Line

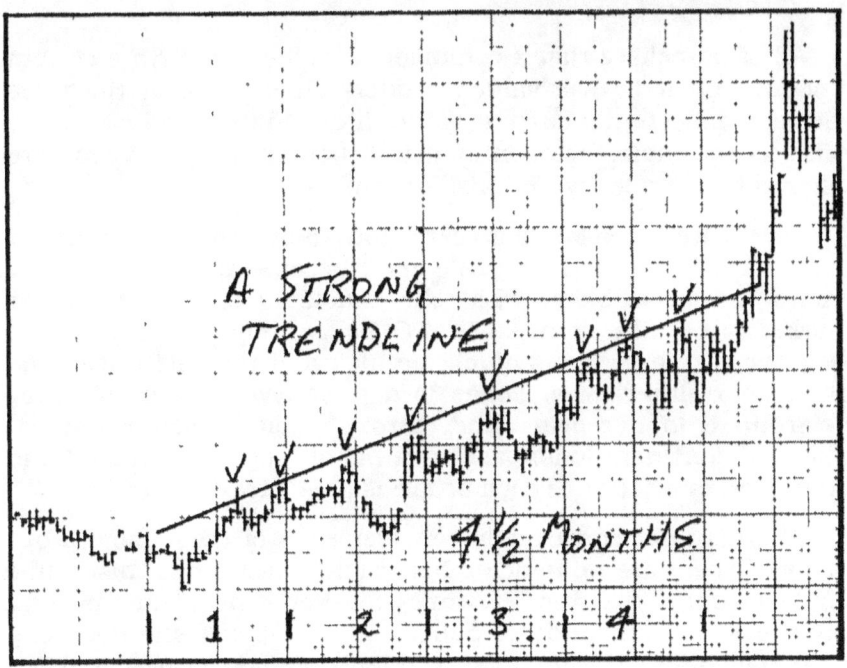

Figure 3-11. This excellent example of a strong trend line illustrates a couple of important points. The line of resistance held through 8 separate price onslaughts as the market came up to the line and bounced off. It also remained unbroken for 4 1/2 months before a breakout finally did occur. Once the line was broken the price change was immediate and dramatic.

Strategies

There are two basic approaches used in the trading of any market item - be it a commodity, stock, or can of beans in the supermarket.

Chapter 3

1. Price level

All of us believe that a commodity or stock is worth a certain amount and it is over-valued, under-valued, or that the price correctly reflects it's current value. Individuals who look at the price as the main factor influencing their trading decisions are referred to as price-level or position traders.

Mrs. Jones goes into a grocery store to buy some groceries for the weekend. She seeks out sale items because they are currently trading at levels below what she considers to be the regular market value. She spurns DRIPPO Coffee, though, because she feels the regular price is much too high and the sale price is no great deal either. Mrs. Jones is a price-level trader. She has determined in her own mind, through comparison shopping, seasonal considerations, past price history, current demand and other factors what price each article is presently worth.

She may not consciously consider each of these factors but many of them are influencing her trading decisions. This is fine for Mrs. Jones because it works for her. She is not putting hundreds or thousands of dollars on the line if she does buy DRIPPO coffee. If the price suddenly comes crashing down because there is no demand for an overpriced instant coffee it is no catastrophe.

Mr. Jones, on the other hand, is also a price-level trader, but he is involved in the commodity markets. If he feels that coffee is **underpriced** he may decide to **buy** a futures contract or two of coffee. He doesn't buy a tin of DRIPPO or any other brand, though, he buys 37,500 lbs. of coffee per contract. For each cent of price change per pound of coffee Mr. Jones either makes or loses $375 per contract.

He can also do something that Mrs. Jones cannot. If he feels that coffee is **overpriced** he can **sell** contracts on the commodity market and make money as the market comes crashing down - if it does. He can just as easily sell a contract at a high price and buy later at a lower price as he can buy and sell in reverse order. Mrs. Jones can only buy and so looks for bargains. Mr. Jones looks for any commodity which he believes is currently under-valued or over-valued. He can make money as it goes up or comes down.

2. Movement

The movement trader considers the price of a commodity to a lesser degree than the **trend**, or direction, that prices have taken over the last few days and months. He feels that there is an overwhelming tendency for prices to continue in the direction they have been heading and to build momentum as they follow that trend. The movement trader **first** looks for patterns and the development of trends and **then** considers the relative price of the item, be it a stock or commodity.

Mrs. Nelson shops at the same grocery store as Mrs. Jones and also sees that DRIPPO coffee is on sale. She knows that coffee has been going up in price lately and feels that it will probably keep going up until some big change occurs. Since it is on sale she feels that it is a good time to buy some because the regular price is only going to be higher the next time she comes shopping, anyway. She also feels DRIPPO is high but reasons that it is likely going to go higher before it drops in price. She is a movement trader.

The Trouble With Bargains

Most traders like to shop for bargains. The trouble with bargains is that they usually become even **better** bargains after you buy them. Trend, as we have seen, is the overriding factor in influencing the direction a market takes. Once a market is in a downtrend it takes a major change in market sentiment to get it going the other way. Many investors feel it shows strength, sophistication and market savvy to ride out a poor performer until it turns around.

One problem with waiting for such a turnaround is that it ties up any capital you do have left for an indeterminate length of time. This is time and money that could be better spent looking for active markets with good profit potential. Leaving your money tied up with a loser just because you happen to own some shares or futures contracts does not make sense.

Chapter 3

Some people feel that a loss of equity is only a paper loss until the stock is sold or the futures position exited. They use this as justification for hanging on until the market turns around and they can recoup their losses. When this happens they are traditionally happy with breaking even. Profits are unimportant by then; all they want to do is get back the money they had and not incur any "real" losses.

What they are really doing is keeping their focus on a market with little immediate profit potential. It is difficult to admit, but a "paper loss" is real. It is no different from selling one loser and putting the remaining money into another one at the same price. In the end you are in exactly the same position.

If it helps change the name on the stock or commodity you should have abandoned long ago, take what money remains, and go looking for a market that you can trade profitably.

Technical versus Fundamental

The information that traders consider in making their trading decisions can be broken into two basic areas:

1. Technical and 2. Fundamental.

Technical information refers to the use of charts, trendlines, and various systems of trying to predict what prices are going to do based on past behaviour.

Fundamental information refers to available knowledge about any factors that may be influencing the prices of various commodities or stocks. In the case of commodities this would include world weather patterns, economic considerations, supply and demand information, world politics, instability of military dictatorships, etc., etc. The list can go on endlessly. With stocks it would be the economic and business considerations of the company in question.

Most traders use a combination of these two types of information to make their decisions. The problem with strictly fundamental factors is that there are so many of them influencing the price of almost any market that the average person cannot hope to have a good grip on the global picture as it effects the price of wheat, or IBM shares, for that matter.

The trader who leans toward the technical side, as I do, does not necessarily worry so much about **what** is affecting the price of commodity or stock but, rather, **how the price is reacting** to the sum total of all influencing factors. This is why trend is so important. If the various factors tend to support the price of a stock or commodity and push it even higher a trend is established.

The more pronounced the trend, and the strength of the underlying support, the greater the momentum that develops. Hop on board at the right time and you can make a windfall riding it for as long as the market continues in the same direction. The thing to remember is that **eventually it will turn around** and that is the best time to get off.

The big challenge is proper timing.

Market Psychology

The line on a chart is a graphic picture of the totality of people's reactions to the **perceived** strengths and weaknesses of whatever is being charted. A stock or commodity has no "value" other than what people are willing to pay for it. Gold has a production cost which has little to do with what it is worth from one year to the next. It is worth what the market, consisting of the sum total of all hopes, fears, perceptions, and beliefs around the world, decrees it is worth.

Each line on a chart represents a universal psychology. The "universe" in each case is a group consisting of everyone that is a participant in that particular market. Each stock, commodity, fad, or concept has a universe of individuals and institutions with attention focused on that market. Some are actively involved, others are mere observers. The observers are watching to see what happens. Some are watching for certain signals before they too become participants.

Chapter 3

What all of this boils down to is the fact that patterns on paper give us a picture of the total market psychology. This psychology can be just as predictable as human reactions in **some instances**. Become familiar with **patterns** which have shown typical actions and reactions over and over again in the past and you have a key to the future.

History repeats itself. Patterns repeat themselves. Watch for patterns and get to know the ones that offer the best potential for predictability. Keep track of the ones you trade successfully and why. These become your **tradeable patterns.**

Narrow the Field

The first thing I do when considering an investment in any commodity or stock is to look over the current charts. I flip through them initially looking for one thing - tradeable patterns. **A tradeable pattern is any pattern which I know from past experience offers good potential to make money.**

I have two favorite tradeable patterns, each with variations, that I watch for:

1. a **breakout from an established range**, and

2. **Sequential Waves** moving in the direction of the long term trend.

Based on these patterns I select the commodities or stocks I am potentially interested in. **All of the markets** are considered at this stage and I narrow the field based strictly on this technical analysis of tradeable patterns. This process culls out at least 90% of the thousands of available markets and accomplishes one of the most difficult tasks to confront a trader - **selecting those that offer the best opportunities to make money.**

After I have narrowed the field using technical analysis then I consider fundamentals influencing each particular marketplace. Based on this important, additional information I decide which markets to trade, how large a position to take, and whether to get in slowly, in stages, or with one order.

Trading Intelligently

We are seeking markets demonstrating patterns that we are familiar with, trends that can be followed, and fundamental considerations that support our predictions. And **we only get in after the market proves us right.**

Getting rid of the riff-raff and concentrating on the few markets with good potential to make you money is the first and most important step in picking a winner.

Markets selected in this way may not move every day or may not even make the biggest moves **but they do represent the ones that can be traded in an intelligent, business-like manner.**

Suddenly there is order amidst the chaos.

Chapter 3

Summary

1. **A line is a line, is a line.** Regardless of what particular stock or commodity the line on a chart represents it is a record of market psychology influencing past prices and can be used to predict future prices. Learn how to follow it and profit from it, with the right frame of mind, and you can make money.
2. **Spot the trend of a market by drawing in trendlines.**
3. Any time a medium or long term trend is violated **a fundamental change has occurred in the psychology of that particular marketplace.** This is an important signal.
4. Two factors indicate the strength of any trend line:
    - **length** of the line and
    - the **number** of times the market has **touched the line** and bounced off.
5. There are two basic approaches used in the trading of any market item:
    - **price level** - watching for value
    - **movement** - watching for momentum

    Trade with momentum
6. The information that traders consider in making their trading decisions can be broken into two basic areas:
    - **technical** - watching for trends
    - **fundamental** - watching for news and information
7. A stock or commodity has no "value" other than what people are willing to pay for it.
8. Patterns repeat themselves. Watch for **tradeable patterns.**
9. Trade **all the markets** but **only a few patterns**.
10. Get rid of the riff-raff. **Discard the vast majority of potential trades.**

Chapter 4

Trade Patterns Successfully

Price Patterns

Commodities and stocks trade in response to the opposing pulls of supply vs demand. Imagine the line on the price chart with two strings attached to the current day's price. One string goes **up** to a white-gloved hand marked "**DEMAND**" and the other goes **down** to a hand marked "**SUPPLY**". The two hands pull at the price suspended in mid-air ... up, down, up, up, and down. If demand is stronger than supply the line goes up, and if supply is the stronger of the two the price goes down. The pulls of the two hands do not necessarily have to represent actual factors of supply or demand; they can be based on the **perceptions** of the market players.

Market players are trying to guess how strong these factors will be in the future and thereby predict which way the price will be pulled. Therefore perception comes to play a large role in determining the trend of any market. If enough people think that the price should go up and start buying based on this perception they create a demand which eventually **does** drive up the price. It will probably not be immediate but it is just a matter of time.

The price chart is a graphic record of the past pulls and tugs in either direction. Some markets are all over the page, others are narrow lines going up, down, or sideways, and others are like a roller-coaster going up and down, up and down...

Chapter 4

Business Decisions

If a market is ranging $2,000 or $3,000 a day (per contract of silver, for example) and is all over the page it is a difficult one to trade. You may have "good" information that the price of silver has nowhere to go but up. Your best friend may have recently bought 10 futures contracts on hope that it does go up. Your broker may be calling you every half hour begging you to get in now before it takes off. But does this mean that you must get in right now? What if you don't and end up missing a good thing?

Remember this - there will always be other markets to trade. Your first and foremost business decision should be that of ruling out those markets which do not offer a good chance to make money.

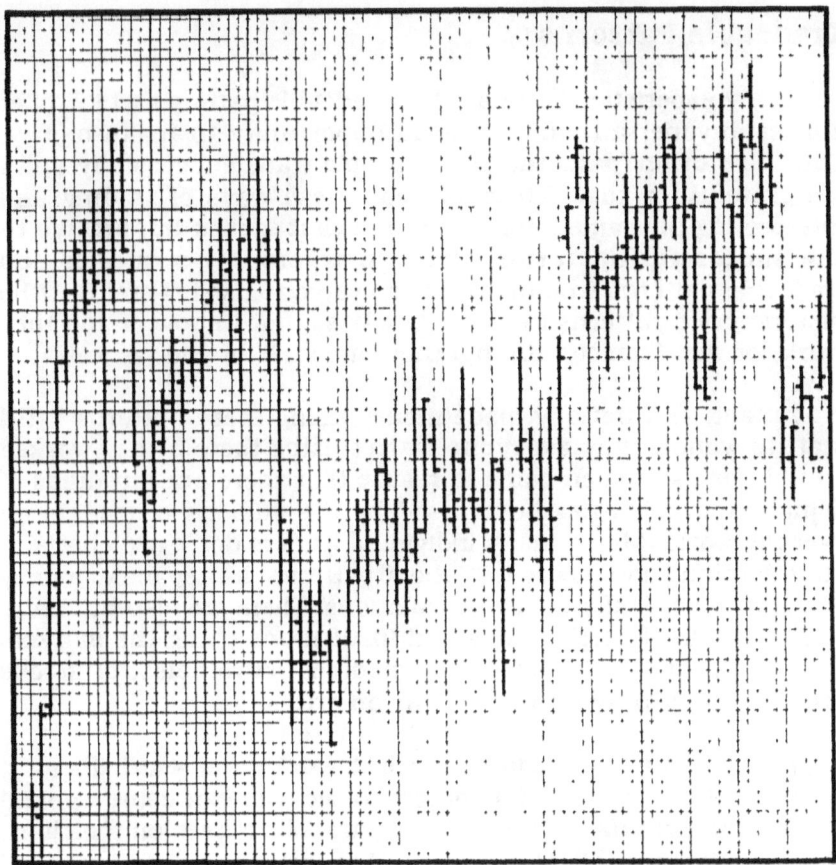

Figure 4-1. *Example of a price pattern which is "all over the page". This sort of market is difficult, if not impossible, to trade with a reasonable chance of making profits. Stay away from all patterns that do not offer good locations for stop orders even if everyone else is telling you to get on board!*

If $2,000 is half of your investment capital you would be crazy to get into the type of market illustrated in figure 4-1! You **could not** enter such a trade without risking all your money and more. Considering the circumstances this is not a tradeable pattern at this particular time.

Managing your own account is a business. Trades must be entered into in a business-like manner - not based on hope, rumour, or emotion.

Chapter 4

Tradeable Patterns

In my experience there are two tradeable patterns which offer almost anyone, anywhere a good opportunity to make money. There **are other patterns** which people trade successfully and I am grateful for that. There are countless ways of trading and interpreting the same information and **that fact is imperative to the successful operation of the markets**. My strategies and tradeable patterns wouldn't work if everyone used them! But the historic price patterns I use are **the best** that I know of and they **work for me**. I am certain that they can work for you, as well.

In fact, as I initially made money using these patterns I **did** start to wonder why **everyone** wasn't using them if they worked so well for me. I soon came to realize that there are hundreds of signals and strategies being used by the millions of traders all over the world. Many, many individual traders don't use charts to start with and could care less about patterns. If they make money good for them; I offer my congratulations. There are also hundreds of thousands of corporations and institutions using the markets to hedge positions in actual commodities, currencies, or stocks and they enter trades based strictly on prices.

In the end all that counts is **what works** and **what doesn't**. Successful trading is not a contest to see who can come up with the longest formulas or the fanciest parabolic curves on the chart. The results are all that count; the return on the original investment. If I find a system as easy as adding 2 + 2 = 4 and it makes money then I am interested. In fact the simpler the better - **if it makes money**.

I don't get in and out of trades every day. I don't speak to my broker each day. **I do watch the charts and update my position each day.** My goal is to make the most money I can, not to make the most trades. In fact, over trading is one of the most harmful and expensive habits a trader can acquire.

The patterns I use are easy to recognize, are simple and straightforward, and allow me to **throw out more than 90% of the potential trades**. As I have repeatedly mentioned selecting the right market to trade is the **first step** to the successful management of my account; but it is still only the first step. The rest of the story is learning **how to trade these patterns.**

An Established Range

As the line progresses across the page with time it can only go up, down, or sideways. We have seen how trends in one of these three directions are formed by markets as they respond to the opposing pulls of supply and demand.

Draw trend lines on any chart and you can define the range over the last 3 months, 6 months, a year, or whatever. If a trend line has been established over more than 3 months it is a long term trend line. This means that it has not been violated for what I consider a meaningful period of time.

Remember the two main factors which indicate the strength of any trend line: the length and the number of peaks or troughs touching it.

Strength in a trend indicates an established range. This strength has been demonstrated by the market; it is not something we have dreamed up or proven with tenuous mathematical formulas. A strong trend line is established for all to see and it **means something**. A price can come up to a trend line which has been established for 2 months, or 4 months, or 6 months, just touch it and then bounce off as if it had hit a wall. We may not be able to explain why, but often **it does**! Sometimes it seems almost uncanny that a price, after several weeks of meandering off on its own, can come up to such a line on a chart, touch it, and then bounce away again.

Chapter 4

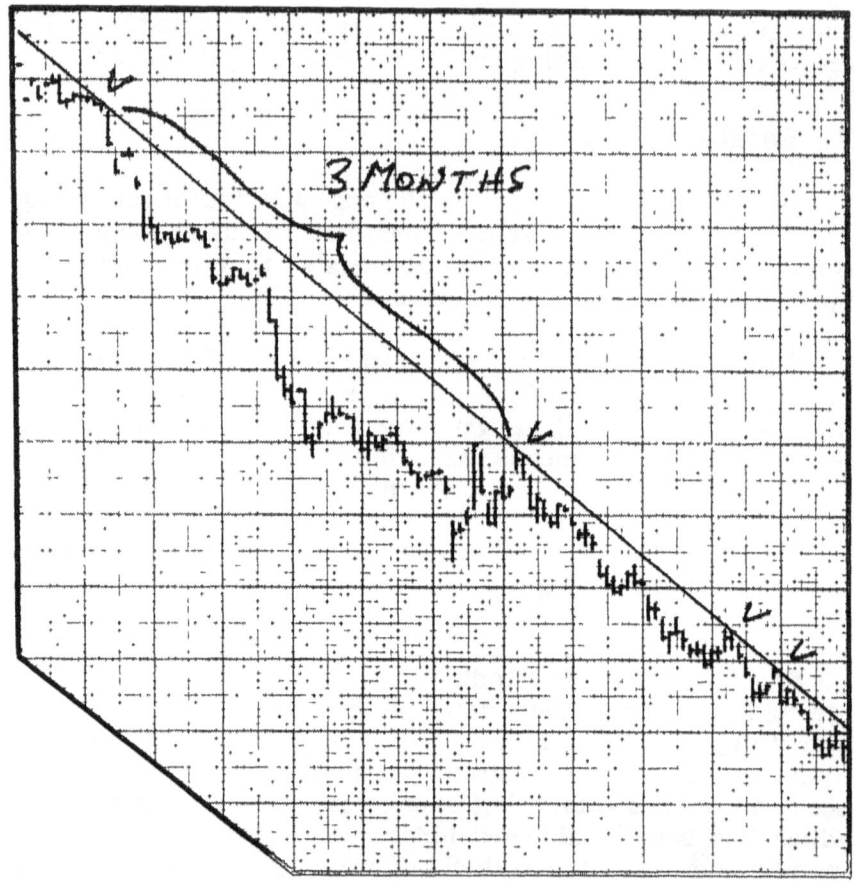

Figure 4-2. This chart illustrates a trendline which obviously means something. After a three month period the price returns to the line three more times to test it before a breakout finally occurs.

Pattern # 1:

The Breakout Strategy

You have come now to the most important statement in this book.

> **THE BREAKOUT STRATEGY**
>
> **When a price breaks out of a stable, established range, for whatever reason, the odds are high that it will continue to move in the same direction.**

The **stronger** the trendline broken the better. Historically we know that if a strong trendline is broken and the price moves out of an established range **something drastic has happened to the psychology of the marketplace.** We may not know what it is; it will probably be a combination of influences or events. But, whatever the reasons, any pull strong enough to break a long term trendline and carry the price into new ground is **usually** strong enough to continue pulling the market in the new direction to establish a new trendline.

This is the basis of what you need to know in order to make money on the markets. The rest is experience, a business plan or system, and the right attitude. There is a lot of other information that should be considered but this simple statement holds the key to a reasonable second income on the markets. And perhaps even financial independence.

The odds that a market will continue in the direction of a breakout are high but, of course, there **are no guarantees**. Remember, this is not a golden rule; it is a pattern which has been repeated many, many times in the past and will be repeated many more times in the future. It gives us something tangible to look for when considering the hundreds and thousands of potential trades we could enter into.

Everything I have said about the breakout strategy applies to markets in which the price is **falling**. In commodities it is just as easy to sell as it is to buy. With stocks it is a little more difficult. But do not forget that **selling short** presents just as good an opportunity to make money as **going long**.

Chapter 4

By selling short I mean selling with the expectation that the price will go down so that you can buy at a lower price later on. Many traders with stock market experience have a mental block against selling short and this can limit your profit potential in trading, particularly on the futures markets. This will be explained in greater detail in an upcoming chapter. **Don't forget to trade from the short side as well as the long.**

The Breakout strategy is not new and it is certainly not original to me. Many people are aware of this principle and even use it in their own trading but few have the account management tools needed to make this signal the basis of a system for making a lot of money. The total package is not difficult to understand, is not complicated, and can be readily applied in the real world. Even so very few people have learned to profit from it on a regular basis.

If you have the time, the energy, and the inclination this simple concept can change your life. Learn to apply it patiently, and without greed, and you will have a talent few people even dream exists; a money making skill that many people pay thousands of dollars to possess.

SIDEWAYS CHANNEL

Most traders just yawn when they see a sleepy sideways channel but whenever I see a very quiet market going along sideways in a tight channel I get excited. I **know** that eventually the price will break out of the channel. And when it does the odds will be great that it will continue to move in that direction with a lot of vigour. The longer and tighter the channel the better; the eventual move should be all that much faster and more forceful.

This is, in my experience, **the most tradeable pattern** to be found in any market. This is my favorite because it tends to be the easiest market to trade and also the one that creates the greatest profits. If you restricted yourself to trading only this one pattern you would probably do better than 90% of the traders involved in the markets!

Trade Patterns Successfully

Initially I thought that channels must be a rare occurrence and that it would be difficult to make money waiting for such an infrequent pattern. What I found was that these channels occur at least half a dozen times a year in the commodity markets and many, many times a year amongst the thousands of stocks.

It **does take discipline** to wait for channels and there is always a tendency to overtrade in a hurry to make a fortune. I think this is the greatest danger for any trader. A few successful trades tend to make the trader overconfident and he thinks he is "better" than the market. The typical reaction becomes, "Why wait for channels when I could be making money faster by forecasting more trends and trading all markets much more aggressively?".

The result of this type of thinking is that too many risky trades are entered without real consideration for what could happen if the market turned around. The trader feels invincible for a short while and then wakes up one day to realize that a few larger than necessary losses have frittered away most, if not all, of his previous gains. It seems that all successful traders have gone through this scenario. If a trader survives this period, and learns his lessons well, I think he becomes more effective and cautious because of it and even more successful in the long run.

Chapter 4

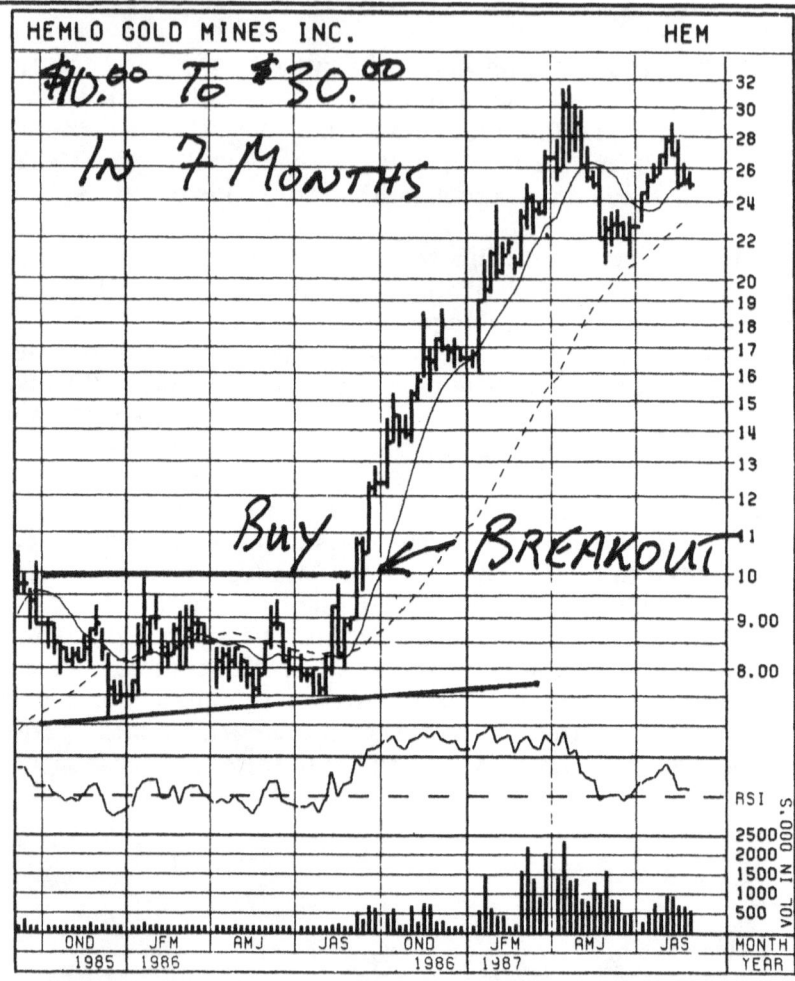

Figure 4-3. On this weekly chart **Hemlo Gold Mines Inc.** breaks out of a sideways channel and goes from $10.00 to $30.00 in 7 months. $10.00 had been a level of very strong resistance. By placing a resting buy order at around $10.25 - $10.50 a trader would have stayed out of the market until it started to move. Another good example of the type of action that usually occurs after a breakout.

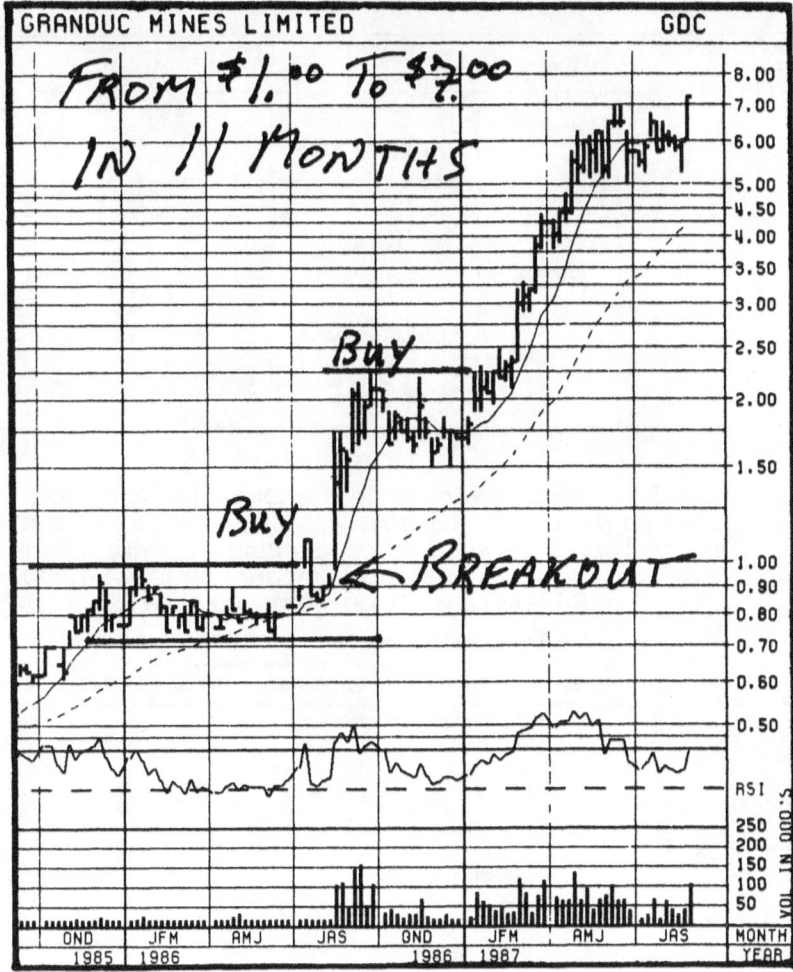

Figure 4-4. *Granduc Mines Limited* makes a run from $1.00 to $7.00 within one year of a breakout from an eight month established range. A short area of congestion below $2.25 offered a second excellent opportunity to enter the market.

Chapter 4

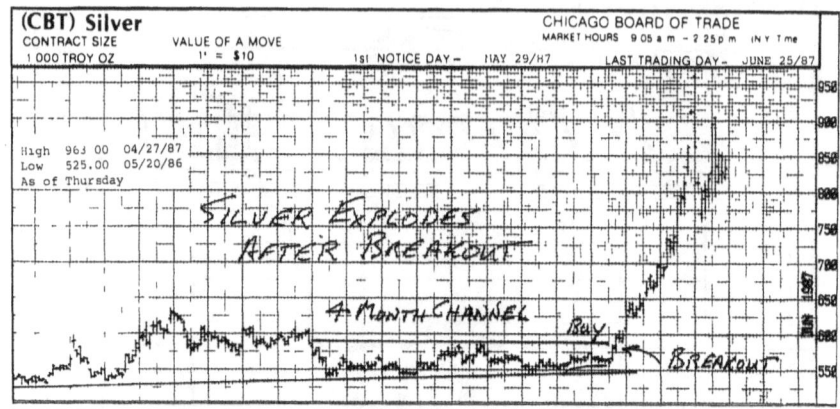

Figure 4-5. This picture is nice enough to frame and hang on the wall! After a perfect four month sideways channel (and an even longer sideways trend) silver breaks out in early 1987 and embarks on a run away climb from $6.00 to over $9.00. Were you in on it?

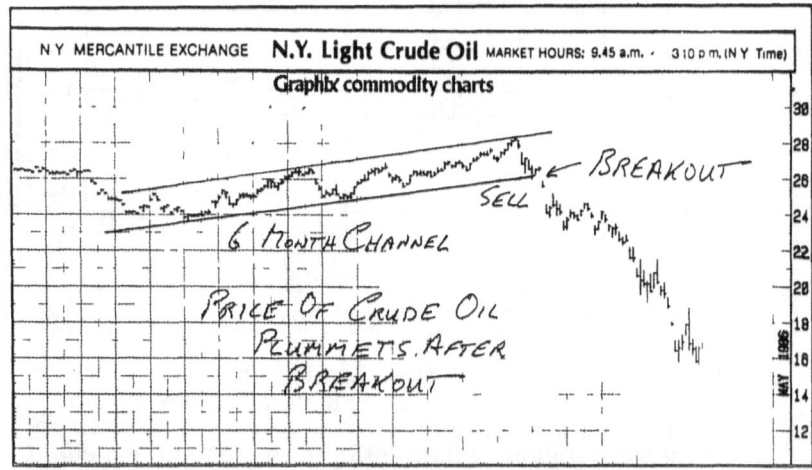

Figure 4-6. A perfect opportunity to sell short. Crude oil is trending very gently upward and sideways in a tight channel formation when it suddenly peaks and breaks past the six month line of support. A signal to the trader to watch carefully! It just kept on dropping and went from $26 to $16 in 2 1/2 months.

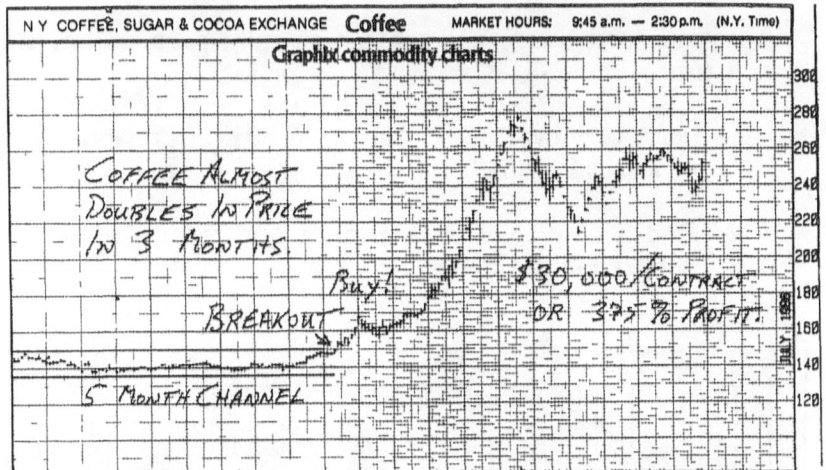

*Figure 4-7. Coffee makes a breakout from a long sideways channel and goes on to almost double in price within three months. This one move could have rewarded the trader with a profit of $30,000 CAN on a $6,000 investment. Moves like this occur **every year!***

Surging Markets

When a market has made a strong move and broken through an established line of resistance it will often **surge** out of the old range and head for new ground very quickly. This is particularly true of a market which has been in a narrow channel for several months.

I consider a surging market one where the **lows of each consecutive day are higher than the previous day's lows.** In a downtrend surge highs are lower than the previous day's lows.

I have found it profitable to trade surging markets tighter than those in a more usual trading pattern. By this I mean that I watch it much more carefully than I normally would and watch for any signs of a turn around. Surging markets tend to gain new ground in leaps and bounds and almost inevitably reach a point when they are over-bought or over-sold. When people get out of such a market, to take profits or losses, they do it in hordes and the **price tends to retrace some of the previous movement very quickly.**

Chapter 4

After a sudden surge the market usually does one of two things; it can:

1. very, very quickly retrace 40 to 50% of previous gains or losses leaving behind a sharp spike, or

2. find a new level of resistance and form a pattern of congestion in the form of a plateau or flag.

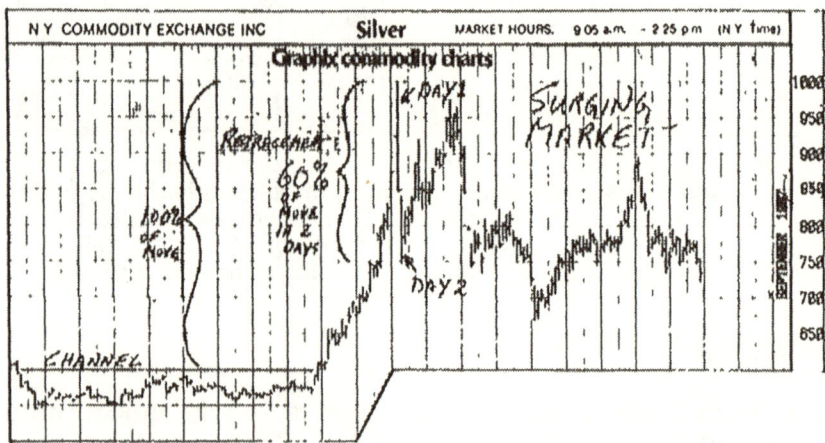

Figure 4-8. A surging market. Looking again at **silver** in 1987 we see how a volatile market can make sudden, unexpected moves very quickly. This late stage is **not** the time to be entering a trade! A good reason for using price charts.

The move made by silver in March - April 1987, shown in figure 4-8, caught everyone by surprise. I personally saw $20,000 in potential profits disappear in about 5 minutes! Silver retraced 60% of prices gained over a 1 month period in 2 **days**. These 2 days caused chaos on the New York Commodity Exchange forcing them to make basic changes to the archaic clearing system in use at the time.

When limit moves start to occur in the commodities market be very careful! Do not try to enter the market at this late stage in the cycle. It is time to either exit the position or stand on the sidelines. Another opportunity may be around the corner...

If the market **does not** suddenly retrace it's move but continues sideways to form a flag or pennant pattern you have an opportunity to trade it once again. This type of pattern is a very **tradeable pattern**. It forms a period of congestion and can be traded as a breakout from an established channel. The price will tend to continue in the direction of the original move; with the long or medium term trend. Place your orders and stop- losses accordingly and you can profit once again as the market continues the move in the same direction!

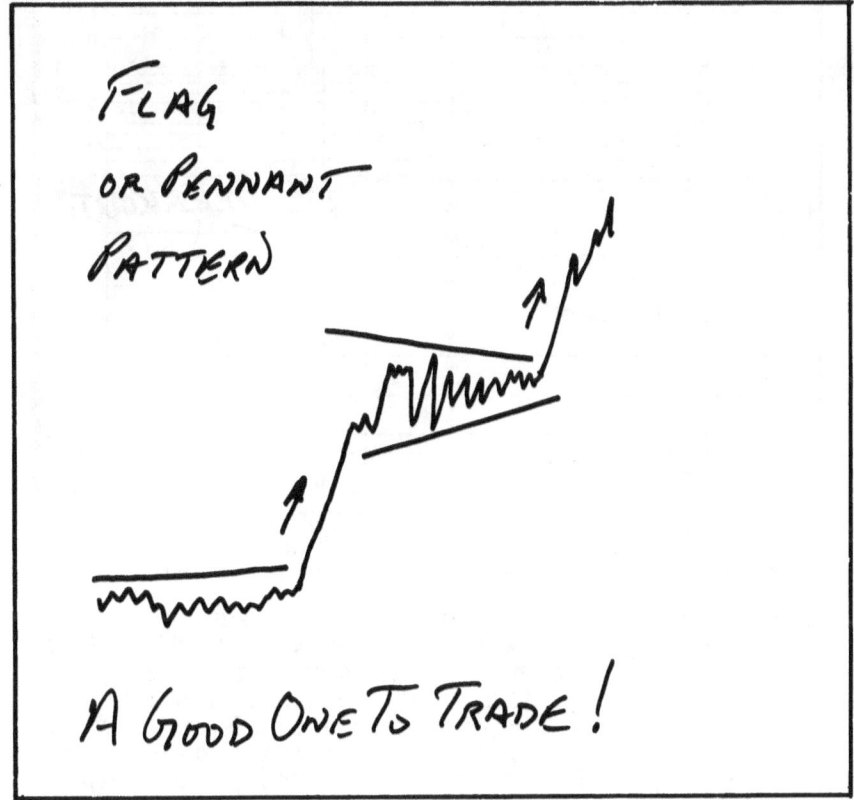

Chapter 4

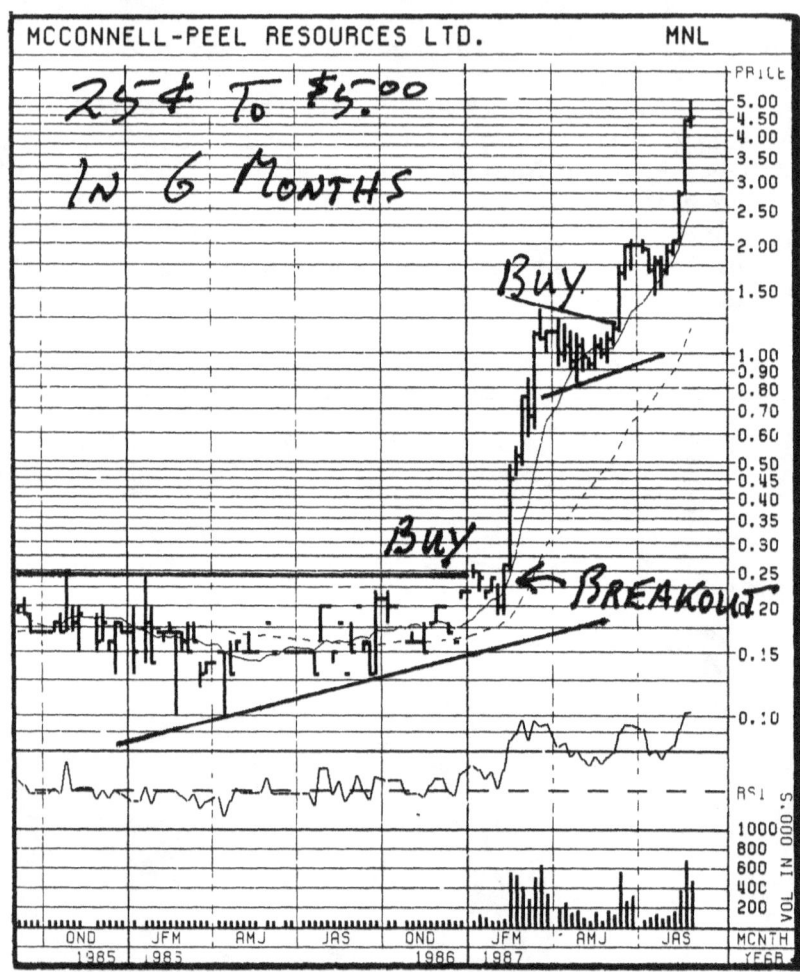

Figure 4-9. Another good example of a surging market; in the stock market, this time. **McConnell - Peel Resources Ltd.** makes a sudden breakout and goes from 25 cents to $1.25 in about 6 weeks. At that level it forms another area of congestion and levels off for 3 months. This offers another excellent opportunity to buy in an uptrend market as it breaks past previous highs. When it does break past $1.25 it races up to $5.00 in only 3 months. It took six months to go from 25 cents to $5.00; almost 2,000% return on the dollar!

A final point about surging markets. Prices can fall even more rapidly than they go up and there are many good opportunities to **sell** on a breakout and ride a surging market down. This is particularly true with commodities where it is **just as easy to sell as it is to buy**! Remember to consider selling on a breakdown of prices.

Pattern # 2:

Sequential Waves

The line on a chart is essentially alive. It is, as we have seen, a graphic representation of mass psychology pertaining to a commodity, stock, or what have you. This wandering line, then, has it's roots buried deeply in human emotions, hopes, dreams, goals, greed, perceptions, etc, etc. We are dealing with a biological entity in many respects.

My own background is scientific. I was originally trained as a biologist and worked for many years in the field. The line on a chart acts very much like an organism trying to get from one side of the page to the other, reacting to various pressures and stimuli as it goes along. Any organism finds its way by using **course correction**; it only gets from A to B by meandering back and forth, going off-course to one side, correcting, going off- course to the other side and correcting...on and on. In the end it gets to B but only **after spending less than 5% of the time heading directly towards it's goal**.

Chapter 4

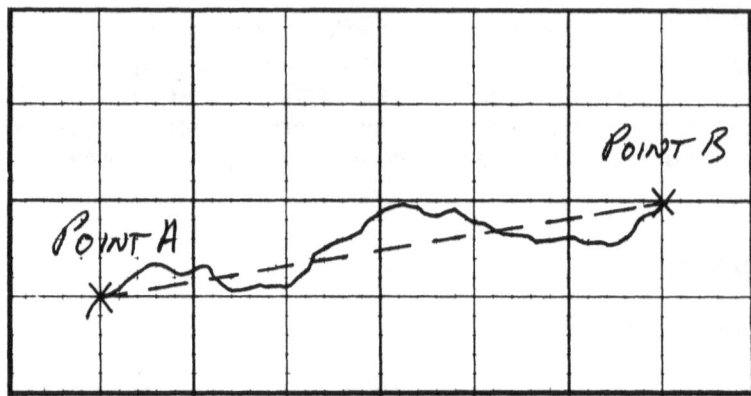

Figure 4-10. A sketch showing how an animal or person might get from point A to point B using **course correction**. Notice that the solid line does not point directly at the target very often and yet it gets there in the end.

If you look at the chart of a market in a definite trend you will most often see a very similar pattern. The line weaves back and forth within the established range, sometimes with the trend, sometimes against it, but unerringly in the general direction it has established.

How do we define a trend in words? An **up-trend** is a market where the peaks and troughs are at ever **increasing** price-levels. A **down-trend** is one where the peaks and troughs are at ever **decreasing** price-levels. The resulting line looks like a series of waves as it climbs or descends with the established trend.

Trade Patterns Successfully

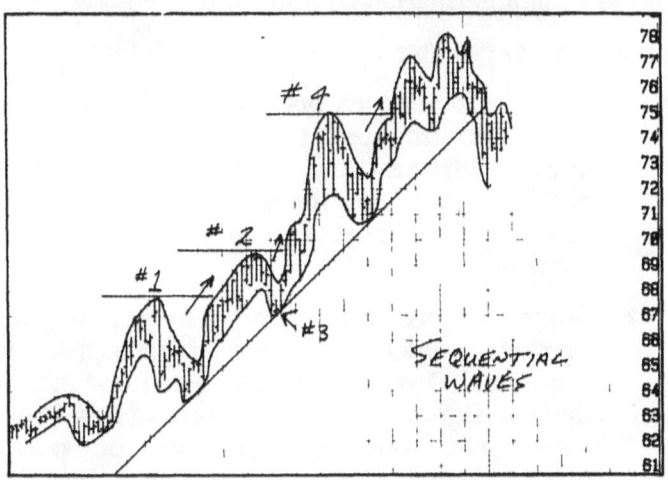

Figure 4-11. Sequential waves in an uptrend market. The price tends to break past a previous peak (#1) to continue in that direction, form a new peak (#2) at a higher price-level, descend to roughly the level of peak #1 to form a trough (#3), and turn up to break past peak #2 to form a higher peak (#4). **As long as the market has enough momentum** *to propel it past each subsequent peak it continues in an up-trend. The boundaries of the wave formation have been drawn in to illustrate the pattern more effectively.*

In an up-trend market a price-level just above the top of the last peak is, therefore, a good location to place a buy order. Similarly, in a down-trend market, the area just below a previous trough is a good location for a sell order.

Stop loss placement in this type of pattern is important. In an uptrend market place the stop loss under each trough in sequence and move it up only when a well defined reversal point shows up. If, at any time, the price breaks down below such a point it is **time to exit**.

In a downtrend market place the initial stop loss above the peak and re-locate it **above** each reversal point in sequence as the market falls away. Once again, if the price breaks above a well defined high it is **time to exit** the trade.

Chapter 4

How can this information be applied to the markets?

Sequential Waves give us the opportunity to:

1. Enter a trade based not on hope or wishes but on the actual performance of the market. Our money is on the line only **after a trend is established** and continues to build momentum in the indicated direction. Why guess at where the market is going when we can wait for it to show us?

2. Stage-in more orders and a larger position as the market breaks the crest or trough of waves in sequence. Our investment increases only when the market signals that it is entering new ground. This allows us to, once again, increase our position **with momentum** based on the actual performance of the market.

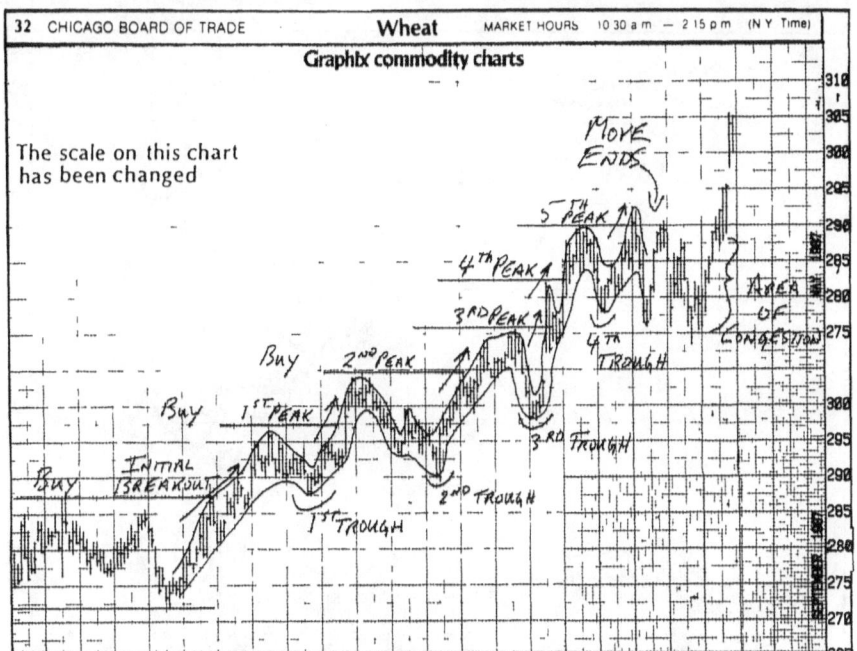

Figure 4-12. *Another example of the sequential wave pattern. Each time a previous high is surpassed the market has enough momentum to carry it to new highs. There is also a weakening of the market after each high and this is the point to wait for in placing stop losses. You can see that the **2nd** trough **almost** broke below the level of the **1st** trough but turned around to form perfect waves. Stop loss placement becomes a fine art and one worth perfecting!*

In both figure 4-11 and 4-12 I have drawn both sides of the line to define the pattern more clearly. This is for the sake of illustration in the book. When I am considering an actual trade I only draw the lines of support or resistance at peaks and troughs, as shown on the following chart.

Chapter 4

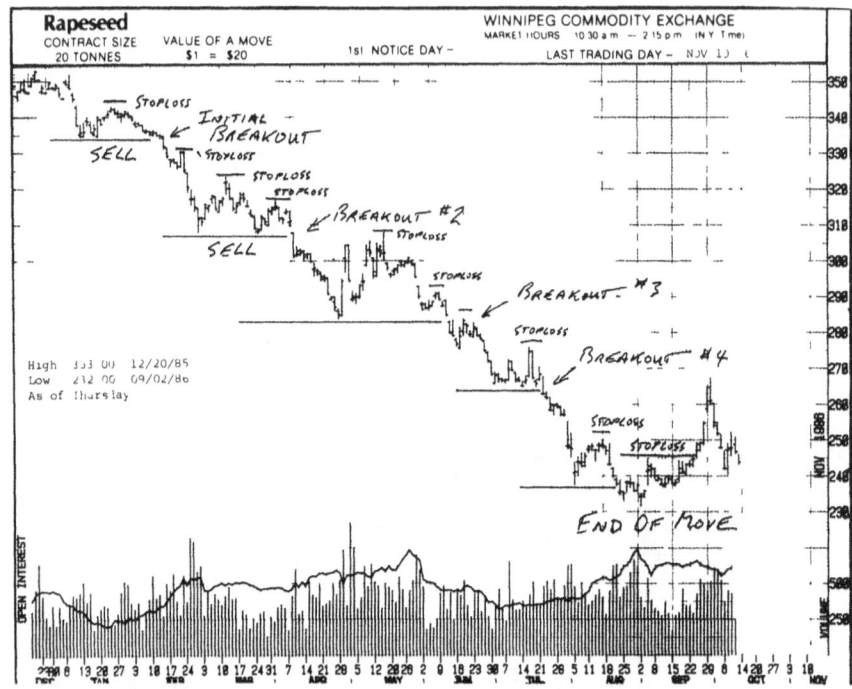

*Figure 4-13. A sequential wave formation in a downtrend market as I would trade it. In this example I have not drawn in the wave boundaries but the pattern is the same as in Figures 4-11 and 4-12. As long as the price continues to break below previous lows the wave pattern remains inviolate. A trailing stop loss locks in the profits as the market falls and takes us out near the bottom. This sort of market is occurring **every day!***

Wave Theories

Many people are familiar with the **Elliot Wave Theory**. Elliot theorized that each business cycle produces eight waves which can be followed on charts for the major economic and stock market indices. This is a valuable tool for an overview of the general economy but becomes difficult to apply to the price of a specific stock or commodity.

When we chart **Sequential Waves** we are interested, not in how many waves there are in each cycle, but rather, in a successful strategy for trading a particular pattern. We are

Trade Patterns Successfully

interested in signals which can be applied to trading a **trending market** with minimum risk of a major price reversal against us. This is important because the amount of risk we are willing to accept is often just a tiny percentage of the potential range of any market, particularly with commodities.

This means that we must have a strategy which allows us to get in on a market which has the potential for a 50% to 100%, or even more, change in value while limiting our risk to **less than a 5% move against us.** An overview of the Dow Jones, S & P, or a major Commodity index will not do this for us.

Percentage Profit

Some people may not like waiting for a move to develop. They would prefer to get in **before** it begins in order to capture a greater percentage of the potential profit. The problem with this approach is that you end up trying to guess **when** a move is about to begin. The chances of guessing correctly very often are not good. If you are right you do have the chance of gaining a bigger profit on the same move but what do you use as a signal to bet hundreds or thousands of dollars on the **hope** that a large move is about to begin?

I would rather take 50% per trade of the potential profits reliably trade after trade, and with much less risk, than take 90% on one or two lucky guesses and then lose all on the rest.

Timing, Timing, Timing

These strategies solve the most difficult challenge of all for most traders, that of proper **timing**.

Many people "know", for instance, that silver will go up in price from it's current levels. Someday it **will** but... when? Will it go down even further before it turns around? How do we know when silver is a good buy? Price level traders would say that it is a good buy right now at current levels (below $5.50 per ounce as I write this in 1986). But the trend right now is still down for silver. There is no concrete evidence that it is going to go up in the near future. Is it really a good buy?

Chapter 4

If we see a breakout of an established range we have a signal that something, somewhere is changing. This is what we are looking for - a signal to let us know when to buy silver based not on hopes and rumours, but on the actual market and real price changes.

A period of stability in a market such as a channel or trend gathers momentum. The longer the period of stability, the more impetus required to cause a breakout from the established range or past previous points of resistance. This means that a breakout from a long term channel or narrow trading range is an indication of a major change in market conditions. Any change strong enough to cause such a breakout has good potential to keep pushing the price in the same direction.

Summary

1. Select trades with high profit potential based on tradeable patterns. Draw in trend lines, decide on the long and medium term trends, and watch for the following important patterns:

    Pattern #1: Breakout from an Established Range

    Pattern #2: Sequential Wave formations

2. A **sleepy sideways** channel forms the most tradeable pattern in my experience.

3. Trade **with the trend**.

4. Use **sequential waves** as one way of staging-in a large position on a market which offers a lot of potential based on all factors.

5. Wait for a move to **develop and then get in**. You may not profit from as much of the move, but you will **profit reliably from many more moves. Take a position based on reality, not on hope.**

Chapter 5

Intelligent Trading Tactics

Intelligent Trading

With the tools and strategies discussed so far in this book you have the ability to considerably narrow the field of potential trades from the thousands available to a mere handful. You have seen how both tradeable chart patterns and fundamental considerations are important for an intelligent approach.

Once a few markets with the proper credentials have been selected you must be able to predict;

1. The **direction** you expect the market to move in, and

2. The **proper price** to buy or sell at

You have identified an opportunity to buy or sell based on strict criteria. This is only the first step. It is a little like being given your first model airplane kit. You sit back blissfully dreaming of the finished plane soaring high in the sky... only to plummet to earth with the sudden realization that the work hasn't even begun.

The bad news is that in order to make money you must enter into the terrible world of reality; of quick moving markets, a certain degree of risk, and hard cash on the line. In order to win in such an environment you require a **system to get in and out of the market quickly and safely**. The good news is that you are holding such a system in your hand.

Chapter 5

This is the time to put your theories and plans to the test. To enter a trade based on **your** own analysis; to commit yourself to a course of action based not on hope, luck, or gambling but on preparation, planning and experience. This requires a system which you can put down on paper and follow just as you follow the rules of the road while driving to work in the morning.

A System

A written set of rules that you follow in your own trading approach makes up your system. At first it is based on a system such as the one I present in this book. Eventually the system you follow will become your own personal trading strategy carefully honed through experience and careful attention to what works and what doesn't.

Rules of Trading

Rules of trading are just as important to your long term survival as the stop signs and traffic lights you encounter on the road. A system does not necessarily have to be complex; but it must be something you can stick with and commit yourself to.

The rules you follow must be written down. This does several things to improve your ability to make money in a business-like manner.

A set of trading rules:

1. makes you carefully analyze techniques that you may be using without much thought.

2. allows no room for impatience or emotion.

3. introduces consistency into your daily trading activities.

4. separates whims and hopes from techniques, and, most of all,

5. it makes you plan for the consequences of every move. A series of steps is developed for you to follow in a methodical, natural order. No more hesitation or feeling lost as you wonder what to do next.

There is no room for changing emotions when making your trading decisions. Every move must be pre-calculated and automatic. You never want to be in the position of watching a stock or commodity go against you day after day, wondering when to get out.

Have you ever been in this position? Have you ever watched profit turn into a loss and then just keep plummeting? Ever sat by the phone, scratching your sweaty palms nervously, trying to decide if you should place that sell order or hang on for **just one more day** to see if it turns around?

Join the club. All traders have experienced the stomach-churning disaster of watching their money trickle away (sometimes on a riptide, it seems) on one trade or another. And most traders continue to trade that way thinking that it is something they have to put up with in order to play the game.

Automatic Entry and Exit

You want nothing to do with this uncertainty and emotional gut-wrenching in **your** trading. Let the market take you in and out at a pre-determined price level - automatically. Use resting stop orders. If your broker is not willing to do this for you I suggest you find one who is. You will both be happier in the long run.

There is absolutely no need for sitting on pins and needles beside the phone and calling for quotes every ten minutes. The most successful traders have long ago discarded such "brush fire" tactics and know they must **plan** their trades and work their system. They have a proper perspective on trading. They are mature enough not to allow such emotions as greed or pride enter into their trading decisions. Above all they are patient.

Chapter 5

If they miss one move they know it is just a matter of time before another good one comes along. The most amazing thing to me in the game of trading is the fact that there are always plenty of opportunities just around the corner. The **sheer abundance of potential money making trades** never fails to amaze me. Successful traders never feel pressured to enter a market before it is too late. With the proper perspective you are waiting for the right move to occur, not waiting for luck to bring you the "hot tip of a lifetime".

Emotion

The system must consist of written rules which you are committed to following - without last minute changes or indecision. As far as I am concerned this is the difference between making an investment and gambling. The investment must meet certain criteria **previously** determined and applied without emotion. A gamble is a toss-up, most often on a whim, with little input from you. You are in control of a trade; gambling offers no such control.

The majority of traders base their decisions on what they read in the papers, what their broker tells them, and what their friends are buying. The most "reliable" source of information for the average investor is the "hot tip". They don't have a picture of the trade in their minds. They have no pre-determined maximum for any loss that they may experience. Timing is, in most instances, based on price-level perceptions; is the stock a good deal or is it not? Present and past trends are usually not even taken into consideration.

Trades approached in this matter are a hit and miss sort of thing. The investor makes money on some and turns around and loses it on most others. Or he may lose right from the start and complain about his bad luck on the markets. It is not bad luck; it is lack of preparation.

Sranko's Rules of Trading

1. Trade only those markets with **good potential to make money**. Be selective based on chart patterns which have worked in the past. Watch for **breakouts** and **sequential waves**.

2. Do not **overtrade**. When you feel confident that you have the market beat **watch out**, a big loss is probably just around the corner. **Keep track of losses** and gains will look after themselves.

3. **Go with the trend**, never against it. Only go against the long term trend once it is broken.

4. Locate a **stop loss** for each position at a pre-calculated level of risk. Never risk losing more than 20% of your account on any one trade.

5. Cut your losses short and let your profits run. Let the **market take you in and take you out**.

6. **Don't** let emotion or impatience enter into your trading decisions.

7. You determine the **price**; let the market determine the **timing**. Use **resting orders** instead of market orders.

8. **Don't count on anything**; only risk as much as you can live without.

9. Winners think about what they will do **if** they lose; losers concern themselves only with what they **could do if they won**. This simply means that winners plan and losers hope.

10. Don't let missed opportunities or profits get you down. There will **always be another good move** just down the road. This is a market of opportunities!

Chapter 5

There it is - your first steps towards having a system in writing. Most of these rules are not original to me. They are shared by many who have pitted themselves against the markets and learned from it. They are the rules I trade by and they have kept me out of trouble in many markets.

Now, let's see how to apply these rules...

Resting Order

Based on the price chart, technical patterns, fundamental considerations, and any other information involved I plan my strategy for each position I take. I very rarely buy or sell "at the market". I use a resting order to get me in and out.

Let's go back to one of the price patterns I recommended that you watch for; the pattern reflecting stability in the marketplace. The narrow trading range or channel.

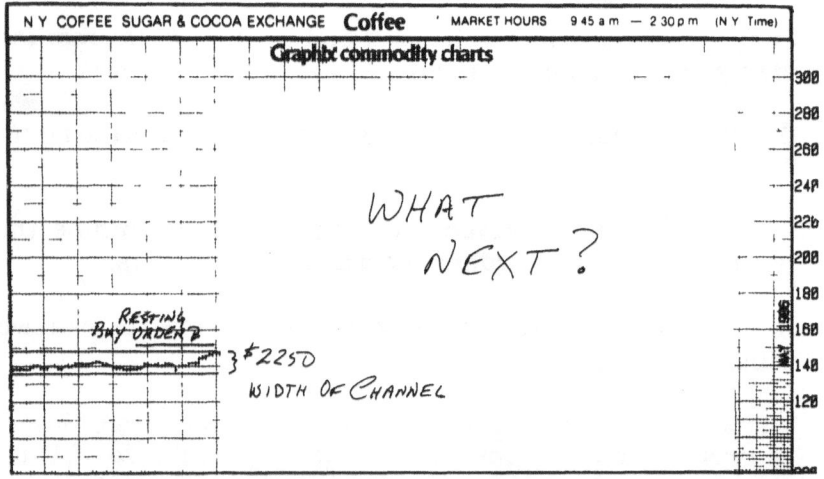

Figure 5-1. **A resting buy order** has been located above the narrow sideways channel on this May 1986 Coffee contract. Based on the width of the channel and change in value (explained in chapter 7) for Coffee ($375 per dollar) I have calculated the width of the channel to be $2250. This means we would be risking $2250/contract by placing the initial stop loss below the trading range.

Intelligent Trading Tactics

The Market Determines Timing

We wait for the price to break out of an established channel as a signal to enter the market. We don't actually sit watching the price ready to put in an order as soon as it breaks out. We leave a "resting order" with our broker.

Precalculate the price that would indicate a breakout and place an order to buy or sell at that price "on a stop". This order is good until you cancel it. That means that it sits there waiting for the market to hit it and then it is filled - automatically.

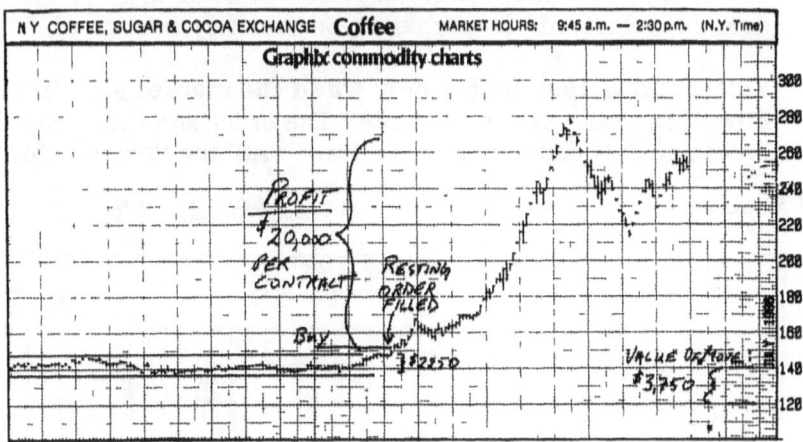

Figure 5-2. A price chart showing what happened to the coffee market illustrated in figure 5-1. As you can see the resting buy order was filled shortly after the breakout and coffee soared to new heights. Each increment of $10 on this price chart is worth $3,750 per contract ($375 X $10). The potential profit from this move was $20,000 US per contract.

Chapter 5

Do you see the importance of a resting stop order?

1. The market takes you in. **You determine the price; the market determines the timing**. Remember the problem with timing? Always wondered how to determine **when** it is a good time to enter a trade? This system does it automatically. Without the emotion of the moment as your broker is telling you that XYZ stock is an excellent buy and you have to "get in right now before you miss a good thing!". Let the market take you in.

2. The market only takes you in **if you were right** in predicting a move. If you predicted that the price was going to go up and it goes down instead; no problem, you aren't even involved.

3. **You invest actual money only when the market goes in the direction you want it to move**. The order sits there waiting but no cash is committed to the trade until the time is right.

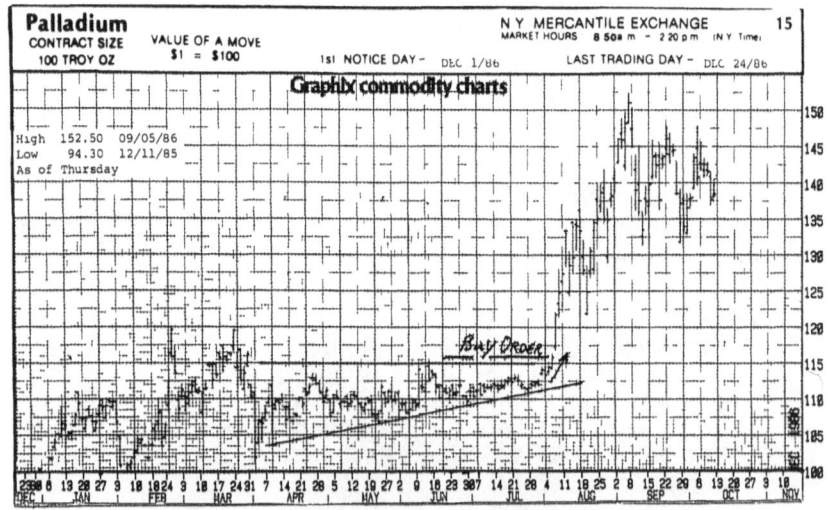

Figure 5-3. On this chart the Palladium market moves in the direction of the resting buy order and it is filled on the day of the breakout. The price quickly jumps from $115/oz. to $150/oz. in less than a month - a profit of $3,500 per contract.

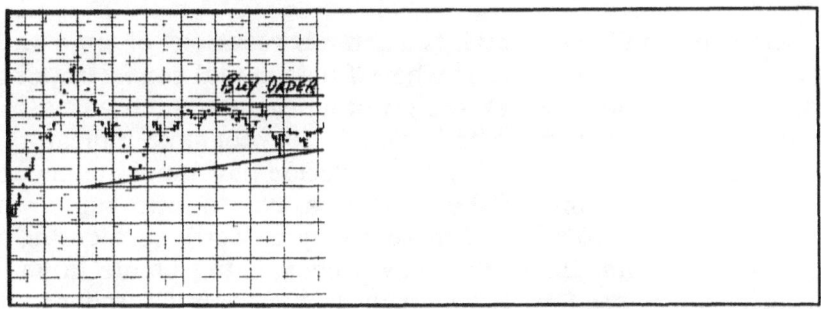

Figure 5-4. Based on fundamental and technical indicators we predict that a price increase will follow any breakout from the established range. A **resting buy order** is placed just above the narrow uptrending channel to catch the breakout **if it occurs**.

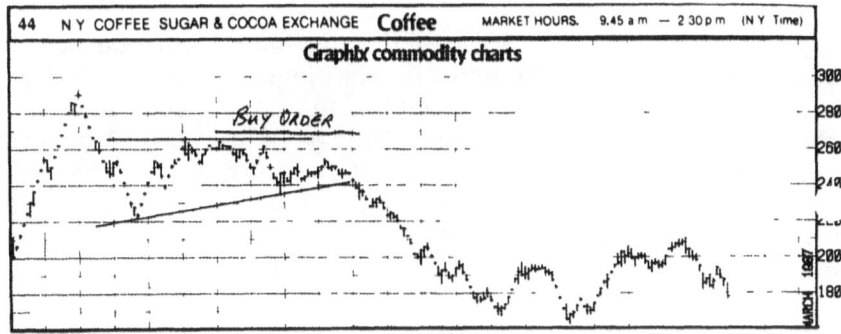

Figure 5-5. Continued from figure 5-4. Instead of going up, as expected, the price breaks **down** through the bottom of the channel and continues to fall rapidly. The market moves in the opposite direction from the stop and the **order is never filled**. No cash is risked. If we had bought on the **hope** that it was going to do what we expected we could have potentially lost our investment.

Chapter 5

Size of the Order

One position is **not worth the same investment of time and money as the next**. This is where fundamental considerations can become important. Based on other factors, such as basis, seasonal indicators, your broker's advice, economic indicators, investment newsletters, etc. you will decide how much money to commit to a position. If the indicators, charts, and your own analysis all point to a strong move it may be worth considering a large trade at that time. But only if **everything** points in your favour. I try to keep my commitment to each position under 25% - 30% of the trading account total.

If you do decide to commit a lot of cash to one trade you will find the sequential wave theory useful in positioning your orders. Position buy and sell stops above or below reversal points as you stage-in the total number of orders you have planned. In this way your investment grows **only** if the market moves in your favour. Your investment remains relatively small until the line picks up momentum.

By scaling-in orders I mean placing more than one order, adding up to the total amount that you are interested in controlling. For instance if I would like to control 5 contracts on a commodity based on a scale-in strategy I could buy 2 on the initial order, 2 on the next, and 1 at the third level. I commit 25%, or more, of my total position to my initial entry point. I find that a larger base position allows me to lock in more of the profits once a move does develop.

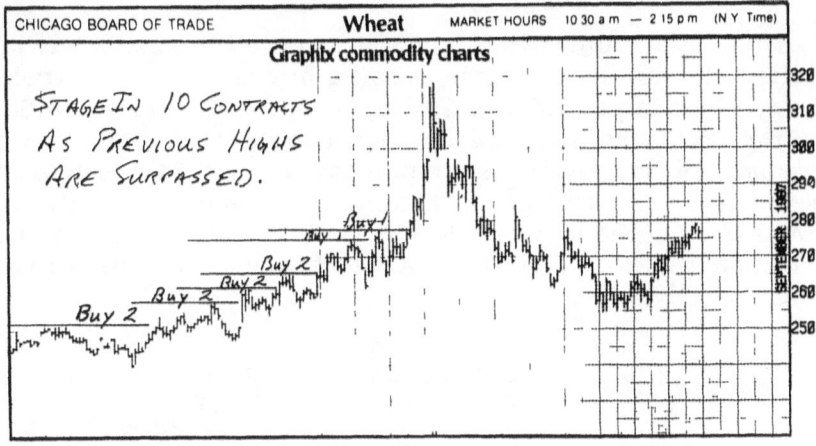

Figure 5-6. *An illustration of **staging** in contracts and increasing the size of our position as the market builds momentum. This strategy ensures that you only end up with a large position if the market swings **strongly** in the direction you predicted. This chart is for the sake of illustration only. In actual practice I would hesitate to enter the market in more than 3 to 4 stages. The average price paid tends to remain too close to the current price and a minor reversal can wipe out all of your profits.*

Remember... Not all positions are worthy of scaling-in large orders. Scale-in large orders only if all indicators point to a strong move in your favour. Scale them in as laid out in the sequential wave theory to take advantage of market signals based on real life, not someone else's opinion.

I have had the greatest success with this technique when I build a strong base position and add to it in only 2 or 3 additional stages as the market moves in my direction. If I get into the market **too late** or try to add to my position in **too many stages** I find that most of the profits can quickly disappear with any reversal in the price.

Chapter 5

Building Pyramids

Avoid pyramiding when scaling-in orders. This refers to starting off with a small order - say a buy order of 1 contract, followed by a larger order of 2, then by 4, and 8, and 16, and... See the problem? You end up with a top-heavy, upside down pyramid. As more contracts are purchased the average price paid goes up and up. Particularly when by far the largest proportion of purchases is at the highest price. It would not take too much of a correction in the market against you, in this situation, to wipe you out completely.

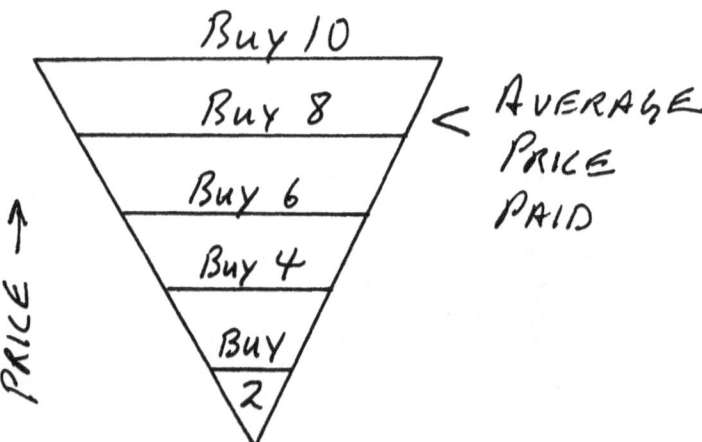

Figure 5-7. An **upside down pyramid**. Notice how high the average price paid becomes and how close to the current price it stays. Not a healthy situation...

If you do decide to scale-in several orders make sure that it is at least a right-side-up pyramid with a stable base narrowing to a lean apex:

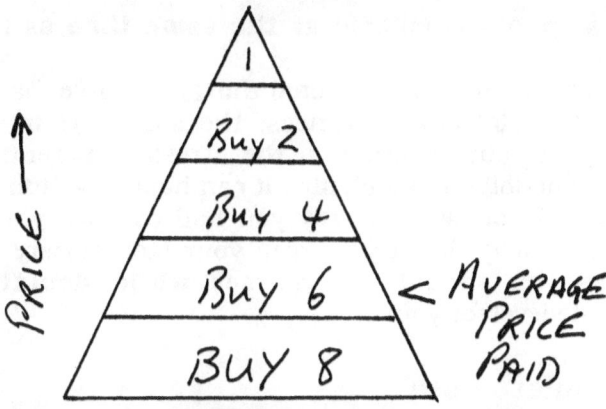

Figure 5-8. A stable **right side up pyramid** with the average price remaining much closer to the base. It is much easier to hang onto profits with this type of structure.

The Stop Loss

Nothing in this world is for certain. Just because the market breaks out of an established range and I say that it will probably continue to move in that direction **does not mean that it will!** The odds may be good but nothing is guaranteed in this market.

A stop loss is nothing more than a resting order to buy or sell on a stop - **but counteracting the original order it is meant to protect.** It is like a safety net in case the market turns against you. This is the order that gives you peace of mind and control over your position.

1. To decide on the initial location for the stop loss you should place it on the **opposite side** of the range from your buy or sell order.

2. If the potential loss at this location is unacceptable **decide on the loss you are willing, and able, to accept and then place your order at the appropriate price level.**

3. If this location is too close to the market and it takes you within the current trading range you **do not belong** in this market.

Chapter 5

4. The stop loss is entered **at the same time** as the original order.

Acceptable loss is a personal thing, of course, based on your present financial circumstances, the size of your investment budget, and your reaction to the stress of potentially losing thousands of dollars - suddenly. It can happen within a matter of minutes and you wonder why you had exposed yourself to so much risk. Why didn't you keep your stop closer? These are questions you should ask yourself **while deciding** on the appropriate level for your stop.

Pre-calculate Loss

In order to determine **where** to place the stop-loss you multiply your position (number of stocks or commodity contracts) times the change in value to give you potential loss for each increment.

For example, if you were considering the purchase of two contracts for the Canadian Dollar you would make the following calculation:

1. change in value = $1000 for each cent per contract (from commodity charts)

2. 2 contracts X $1000/cent = $2000 change per cent. Suppose you are willing to risk $1000 on this trade. This means that you would place your stop loss one-half cent below your buy order. (1/2 X $2000 = $1000).

Consider another example. Say you are interested in buying 500 shares of Fortune Stock:

1. Change in value for a stock always = one cent. (unless purchased on margin)

2. 500 shares X one cent = $5.00 change in value per penny. If you are willing to risk $1000 on this trade you would place your stop loss $2.00 below your buy order ($1000 divided by $5.00 = 200).

Technical Considerations

Correct placement of stop losses is more, though, than pre-calculating the acceptable loss and putting in the order. Take a look at the chart and place your stop loss at a meaningful position on the chart. A **meaningful position** is one that takes the price pattern into consideration.

In placing a stop loss I take two important technical pointers into consideration:

1. The location of **short-term and medium-term trend lines**, and

2. Milestones in the price history as indicated on the chart. **Milestones are points left behind by the line as it makes reversals and then continues in the established trend. These are reversal points.**

Reversal Points

Such points are strong indicators of the market's reactions to current supply and demand pressures. They are often referred to as **points of resistance and support.**

We know that these points indicate prices which the market, for whatever underlying reasons, is reluctant to cross under present conditions. If a line makes a reversal, recovers, and leaves behind a well defined point you have a **perfect location** for your stop-loss.

Chapter 5

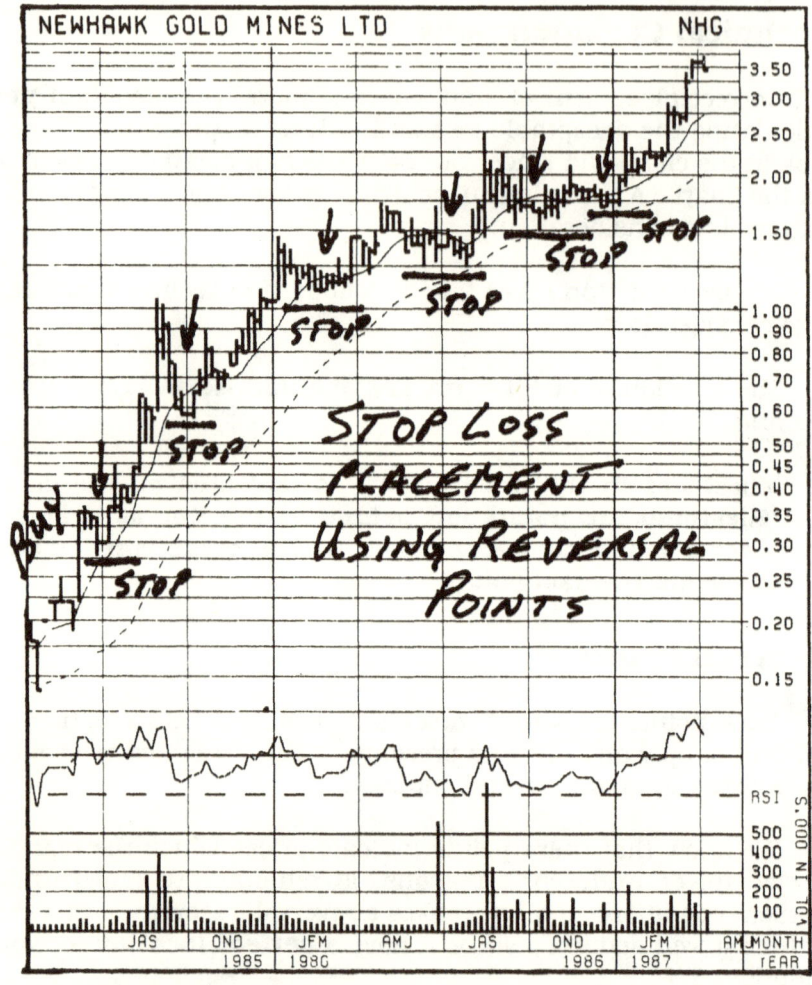

Figure 5-9. Definite points left behind by the market, called **reversal points**, offer reasonably safe and technically meaningful locations for stop loss placement. When such a point is formed it is a sure indication that there is strong and effective resistance or support at that price level. In this case, the sequence of reversal points offers safe resting places for a trailing stop loss.

Intelligent Trading Tactics

Each stop loss has been located a short distance below the actual point and below a price increment on the chart. For example if a point is located at $1.28 the stop loss is placed at $1.23. This is below the point and also below the $1.25 increment line. This simple rule keeps us from being stopped out if the price comes to $1.25 and suddenly turns around but takes us out right away if the psychological barrier of $1.25 is transgressed.

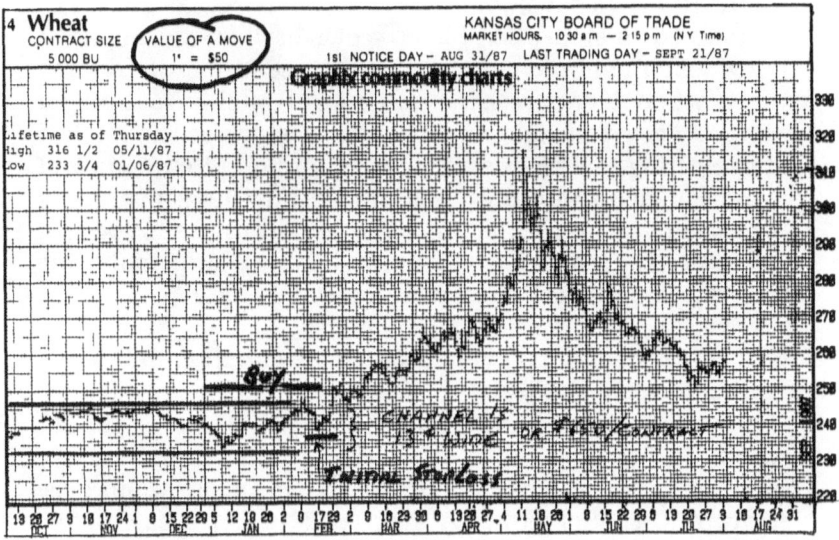

*Figure 5-10. The above chart indicates the location of an **initial stop loss order** based on a calculation of the actual amount at risk, horizontal trendlines (lines of support and resistance), as well as reversal point locations. Referring to the top of the chart the value of a move for Wheat (Kansas City B.T.) is $50/contract for each cent. The channel is 13 cents wide or $650/contract (13 X $50). If we place a buy order and initial stop loss as indicated we are placing $650 per contract at risk. The stop loss is located under a reversal point at a reasonably secure location.*

If $650/contract is **too much** for you to risk on this trade you would not raise the stop loss; you would be wise to wait for another trade which could be entered with fewer dollars on the line. It is that simple. The **primary** consideration in stop loss placement is not how much you can afford to lose but **where can it be securely placed in terms of technical information on the chart?**

89

Chapter 5

The Importance of Automatic Protection

A major factor in the success of this strategy is the use of stop losses to cover any position taken. As soon as I enter a buy or sell order I **simultaneously** enter a counter-acting order at a pre-determined price based on the above considerations.

Consider the average market participant. Call him "El Bravo" for short. El Bravo says,
"Who needs a stop-loss. I keep a close eye on my stocks. I know when I should get out. I don't need an order resting there when I can react much more quickly to sudden market occurrences. And besides a stop-loss is such a static thing. The market is dynamic! Some days I wouldn't give away my position for anything, especially because of some piddley little correction in the market. I say give the market some room to move and make me money. Then I'll get out when the time is right."

Or, if El Bravo is even slightly organized, he may say something like,
"I have a stop-loss in my head. I know it is time to get out when a stock goes down 20%. So I just keep a close eye on it every day and call my broker to get me out when I see it drop 20%. Sometimes I do give it an extra day or two just to make sure it really has turned around and I don't get out too early."

If your system exists only in your head second thoughts become involved at the time of a decision. When the market has gone 20% against you it is probably still moving. The market doesn't pause at this 20% boundary waiting for you to make up your mind.

It is human nature to become possessive of something you "own". Once you have taken a position you become protective of that stock or commodity. A part of it is now yours and you **will not want to give it up.**

Consider this carefully. You have this piece of paper which stands for your interest in a mining corporation, or perhaps in a carload of wheat. It is your natural tendency to want to hang on to this "possession"; tenaciously, doggedly. Emotion takes over and you want to give your position just one more chance. "Just one more day and it will turn around.", you say to yourself. And the next day you say the same thing... and the next day ...

Trade the market this way and you will fail.

You must accept losses, in fact, plan for them by **deciding, even before you enter the trade, where you will get out if it doesn't go your way.**

Remember a couple of the rules at the beginning of this chapter:

1. Let your profits run and cut your losses short.

2. Winners think about what they **will do if they lose**; losers concern themselves with what they **could do if they won.**

This last rule may not make much sense until you lose a couple of thousand on the market and then realize it simply means "Winners plan; losers merely hope." An important distinction and one you must build into your personal trading strategy.

Trailing Stop Loss

Once you have taken a position and the market is moving in your favour you must have a strategy for keeping as much of the profit as possible.

When do you get out? This is a matter of timing, once again. Just as the market got you into the trade you should let the market determine the best time to get out.

I use a technique commonly referred to as the **trailing stop**. This is nothing more than a series of stop losses trailing the current price as it maintains the trend.

Chapter 5

Placement of this series of stop loss orders is more an art than a science. I make use of the same rules for locating each successive stop as I do to determine the initial location.

I place stops by:

1. keeping them trailing **below the trendline**, and

2. placing them **just above or below** a good reversal point with the stop on the other side of a meaningful increment. For example if a reversal point is at 52.40 I would place my stop-loss at about 49.90. If the market drops down to 50.00 and turns around I am still safe. But if it drops below 50.00 I want out.

Some questions may pop to mind. How often is the stop loss moved? How far behind current prices do you keep it trailing? There are no hard and fast rules to moving the position of a stop. It is a lot like reeling in a monster fish - mostly you play it by feel. Some people recommend that you keep it below the lows of the past five days; some say ten. Other people recommend you keep it a certain value behind current prices; 10 cents, $1.00, $5.00 - that sort of thing. Some keep it 5% or 10% below the current day's lows.

I keep my stop trailing below the short-term trend line, sometimes below the medium-term trend. My reasoning is that as long as the market is moving in my direction and staying within the established trend I am happy to go along for the ride. Once it breaks out of this trend, though, I become concerned. Anytime a line breaks out of a well established range it is indicative of some change in the market. I may not know what it is but my interest is certainly aroused.

With a stop just below the trendline I am in the market as long as it continues to make me money. Once it breaks out of the established range, though, I want to be out.

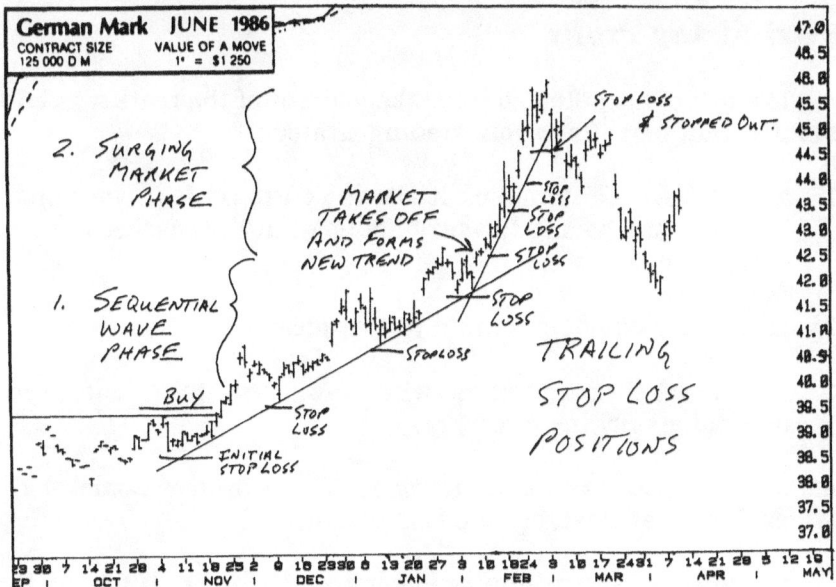

Figure 5-11. *This chart indicates the location of a **trailing stop loss** below both the trend line and definite reversal points. There is no firm rule for stop loss placement and it becomes one of the finer arts of being a good trader. The trendline and reversal points **do** offer two clues for effective placement of the stop loss.*

Also notice the clearly defined sequential waves during the first, slow phase of the move and the surging market during the second, blow-off phase of the move. The stop loss is moved much more frequently during this second phase.

Chapter 5

Maximizing Profit

The use of a trailing stop to take you out of the market results in important benefits to your trading strategy.

1. It is relatively automatic. It allows you to trade in your spare time without having to worry about what the market is doing every minute.

2. Emotion does not enter into your trades.

3. The market determines when you are taken out, you determine only the price.

4. If the market suddenly reverses it will protect some of the profits or, at least, cut the losses short.

Using this system **you will very rarely take 100% of the gains out of the market as profit** (I don't think there is any reliable way of doing that regularly). But **you will take a large percentage of the profits consistently,** one trade after the other.

Surging Market Stop-Losses

I keep stop-losses **tighter** than usual in a surging market. I find that this takes me out close to the top or bottom of a good move and also before the market becomes too volatile.

In my experience it is best to keep your stop trailing close behind the surging market and become stopped out as soon as it slows down. This point tends to be very close to the top of a spike or at the beginning of a period of congestion. In either case you will take the largest percentage of profits by getting out at that point. In this type of market I move my stop-loss every day or two and keep it just outside of the trading range as it moves

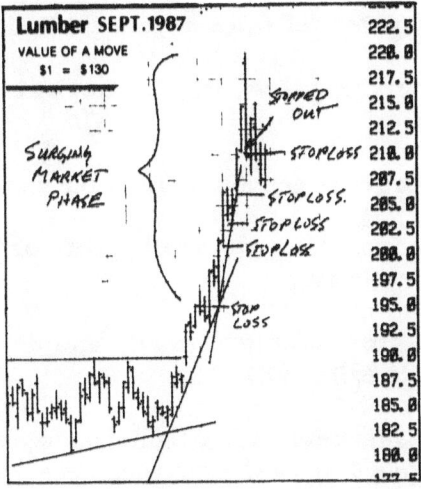

Figure 5-12. Placement of the trailing **stop loss** during a **surging market**. A surging market is defined as one where the low of each day does not break below the low of the previous day, or vice versa in a downtrend market (high does not break above high of the previous day).

The stop loss in a surging market is moved every day or two and kept close to the low of each trading day. If a **limit move** occurs, on the futures market, the stop loss is immediately moved **within** range of the close so that a sudden reversal can stop you out. This phase of the market can become very volatile.

Chapter 5

Summary

1. Use a **written system of rules** in your trading strategy.

2. **You** determine the **price**, let the **market** determine the **timing**.

3. Use a **resting order** to get you in **and** take you out of a trade.

4. Take on large positions by **scaling-in orders** using the sequential wave theory.

5. Use a **trailing stop** to protect profits and determine the best price and time to exit a position.

6. Trade **surging markets** with a tighter stop-loss than normal. On such markets I move the stop-loss every day or two and keep it close to the range established each day.

Chapter 6

Trading Stocks

A Line is a line...

The principles behind trading the line are the same in any market, whether it is stocks, commodities, bonds, or precious jewels. The historical path of prices over time is a representation of market psychology revolving around each particular commodity or instrument of trade, such as a stock or bond. We now know that this historical price pattern **can be used as the initial indicator of a market we should watch closely**. Based on this graphic representation and a few important fundamental considerations we can decide to either enter a trade or not to enter it.

Overwhelming Choice

What we have is choice. In most cases the choices are overwhelming. There are so many potential stocks to trade that the successful trader must come up with a **mechanism for picking winners consistently.** It doesn't really matter what this mechanism is if it allows a person to enter markets with a better than 75% chance of making money.

The mechanism I have been describing in this book is to **wait for the market to start doing what you are looking for,** and **then** get into the action. Hot tips, recommendations, and friendly advice form a part the filter mechanism but are **not the only** things you have to go by.

Chapter 6

How to Trade Stocks

How do I trade stocks? Just the way I trade commodities and any other market I may be interested in. **I look for tradeable patterns.** I place resting buy or sell orders on a stop based on the historical prices, trendlines, points of resistance and support, and important fundamental indicators.

I wait for the market to show me which way it is going and then I **let it take me in**. I follow the market with a trailing stop loss and **let it take me out again**. And then I watch and wait for the next market with a tradeable pattern...

To make money on stocks, as with commodities, you have to decide on two things:

1. The **direction** in which the market is headed. Do you buy or sell?, and

2. The best **time** to buy or sell? How do you determine the timing of your trade?

Seems simple, doesn't it? A successful trade boils down to correctly predicting the direction of a move and getting in and out at the right time. Do that and you will make money. Do it over and over again and you could make lots of money.

Fundamental Factors

Ninety percent of stock market traders rely **too heavily** on market fundamentals. There is **so much** information to be considered for each stock that no individual - no analyst, advisor, broker or trader - can keep on top of it all. Yet this avenue is the one taken by most traders and **it leads in the wrong direction**. Using fundamental information **only** does not give the trader a reasonable means of culling the potentially "bad" trades from the "good" trades.

Trading Stocks

What "Don Guyon" wrote in his book, <u>The Book of Books on Wall Street Speculation</u> way back in 1917 makes just as much sense today.

"To tell a speculator to base his operations on his interpretation of fundamental factors is to leave him just where he started. Most speculators at present try to interpret these factors and fail to do so successfully because they place too much importance on certain factors and not enough on others. **The market itself determines the relative importance of all factors more accurately than any speculator can hope to interpret them**". (Emphasis by the original author).

A lot of brokers and analysts will disagree but they often make their money by making the market seem more mystical and difficult to trade than it really is. If there was a simple way of concentrating on those stocks with excellent potential to make money fewer people would rely on tips from a broker to decide on which stocks to invest in.

Watching for tradeable technical patterns on historical price charts offers us a way of sifting through thousands of potential trades and selecting only those ones with good potential to make us money. **Once a tradeable pattern is selected then fundamental factors can be brought into play.**

Stock Charts

I follow and update stock charts exactly the same as any other charts; by marking in the daily range, trend lines, buy orders, and stop losses. The easiest way of acquiring stock charts is to subscribe to a chart service (such as Independent Survey Company, P.O. Box 6000, Vancouver, B. C., Canada, V6B 4B9) and update only the ones you are following at a particular time. It is unrealistic to try and keep charts up to date on the thousands of potential stocks on the major exchanges. The cost of charts will be more than covered by the profits made available by following a wide cross section of the markets.

Chapter 6

Strategy for Trading Stocks

1. Follow the trend. Never buck the trend or try to outguess the market.

2. Trade patterns not stocks. Consider other factors as well as charts but let the historical price pattern be your **initial and final** decision making filter mechanism. Don't enter a market that is fluctuating wildly. There will always be another, easier one to trade.

3. Place your orders at a pre-determined price-level on a stop and let the market determine the timing. Don't buy and sell at the market, subject to the heat of the moment.

4. Always use a **stop loss** to protect **all positions**. Place stop losses according to what the price is doing by watching the trend line and any points of reversal. Pre-calculate the amount you are willing to lose and stick to it. **Never lower a stop (or raise it on a short position) because you are afraid it may be hit!** If your broker doesn't like to use stop losses get one who does.

Stocks vs Commodities

The stock market may appeal to you if:

1. Your available risk capital is low and you don't have the minimum $2,000-3000 required for trading commodities. You can enter trades on the stock market with only a few hundred dollars.

2. You are not willing to take on the potential risk associated with leverage (buying and selling on margin). I demonstrate how this risk can be minimized but you may feel more comfortable trading without the use of leverage.

3. You are "at home" trading stocks and don't have the time or inclination to learn about a different market and develop the required experience.

Summary

1. **Tradeable price patterns** are the first thing I look for when looking at any market to invest in.

2. **Stock charts** should be used to determine the direction of the general trend and levels of support and resistance for **any** potential trade.

3. **Fundamental** factors form an **important** role in selecting a potential trade, but are secondary to accurate technical information.

4. Use a **stop loss** on all positions.

5. Use **resting orders** to take you **into** the market and a **trailing stop loss** to take you **out**.

6. Find a **broker** comfortable with using resting orders and stop losses. You want to make money and must have a broker who is willing to trade **your** way.

Chapter 7

Trading Commodities

Every day millions of dollars change hands on the commodity markets or futures exchanges. This is the ultimate capitalist marketplace of the world where prices for objects of trade are established through open bid. Instead of bartering over the price of a single animal, bushel of grain, or ounce of silver the game is played with contracts or precisely defined units of each commodity.

This market was set up specifically as an arena for farmers, industrialists, pool operators, etc. - whoever held the actual commodities - to **hedge** their position and transfer the risk of a sudden price swing to the **speculators** who willingly take on the risk in return for potential windfall profits.

Each futures contract represents a train car load of cattle, grain, sugar or lumber, or a fixed value of currency or other negotiable item. The cash value of the contract may be any where from $20,000 to $1,000,000.

Leverage

You may immediately say to yourself, "well, that's the end of it for me... I can't come up with anything approaching that kind of money." Listen. The brokerage firms and commodity exchanges don't require you to pay the full price of the contract; all they require is a margin of 5 to 10%. **You can control $50,000 or $100,000 or even one million dollars worth of goods with anywhere from $1000 to $5000 in actual cash!**

Chapter 7

You can purchase the rights to **any change** in value of $1,000,000 worth of U. S. Treasury Bills, for example, for about $2,000 cash. This is like going to the bank and asking for a $998,000 loan with $2,000 collateral.

Not much chance of success, I would say.

It is an everyday occurrence on the commodity markets. As I sit and write this page I control any change in value of $6,000,000 of Treasury Bills for about $10,000 cash on margin. All bought and sold from my home in British Columbia, Canada.

If the value of treasury bills changes just a tiny amount - only about 0.02% - I either double my money, and put $10,000 in my pocket, or lose the total investment. There is not much tolerance for undisciplined traders in the game of commodity trading.

Change in Value

A price change for in the value of an underlying commodity results in a direct change in the value of the futures contract. This change is value is calculated on the size of the contract and the unit of measure. Consider sugar, for example. If the price per pound of bulk sugar (enough to fill a train car) goes up 1 cent and you own one contract (112,000 lbs.) then you make $1,120. If you own three contracts you make $3,360 each time the price of bulk sugar increases by one cent.

You can also lose the equivalent amount if sugar goes down 1 cent.

Here are some examples showing what a price change is worth per contract with representative commodities:

Trading Comodities

Contract Size and Value of a Move

COMMODITY	SIZE OF CONTRACT	VALUE OF MOVE		
Feeder Cattle	44,000 lbs.	1 cent	=	$440
Live Cattle	40,000 lbs.	1 cent	=	$400
Hogs	30,000 lbs.	1 cent	=	$300
Pork Bellies	38,000 lbs.	1 cent	=	$380
Canadian $	$100,000	1 cent	=	$1000
Swiss Francs	125,000 SF	1 cent	=	$1250
Copper	25,000 lbs.	1 cent	=	$250
Gold	100 T ounces	1 $	=	$100
Silver	5,000 T ounces	1 cent	=	$50
Corn	5,000 bu.	1 cent	=	$50
Soybeans	5,000 bu.	1 cent	=	$50
Soybean Meal	100 tons	1 $	=	$100
Soybean Oil	60,000 lbs.	1 cent	=	$600
Wheat	5,000 bu.	1 cent	=	$50
Orange Juice	156,000 lbs.	1 cent	=	$150
Coffee	37,500 lbs.	1 cent	=	$375
Cotton	50,000 lbs	1 cent	=	$500
Sugar	112,000 lbs.	1 cent	=	$1120
Lumber	130,000 B. F.	1 $	=	$130
Leaded Gas	42,000 gal.	1 cent	=	$420
N. Y. Light Crude	1,000 barrels	1 $	=	$1000
Heating Oil	42,000 gal.	1 cent	=	$420
Eurodollar	$100,000	1 pt.	=	$25
T Bills	$1,000,000	1 pt.	=	$2500

Paper Trades

As a trader on the futures markets you want to earn a profit on the change in value of a certain commodity. You want the profit to appear on paper as a credit to your trading account and as cash whenever you decide to withdraw it. **You do not want to take possession of the physical commodity.** The physical unit of the commodity actually does exist somewhere but as a speculator you are interested only in changes in value. It really doesn't matter to you if you are trading in cattle, gold, soybean oil, sugar or treasury bills.

Chapter 7

It is not the commodity you are interested in; it is our good friend, the historical **price pattern,** and the potential for change in value. Some commodities are more volatile than others and some more predictable - you soon get to know each one - but what they are doesn't really matter that much.

First think about hanging onto what you have and **then** think about making more. Caution is the overriding consideration when trading commodities.

Commodity Labels

Futures contracts are referred to according to the name of the commodity and the expiry date. All contracts expire on designated dates. There are several expiry times or **options** to choose from in each commodity.

Let's look at sugar again as an example. There may be May Sugar, June Sugar, October Sugar, etc, all referring to the month of expiry for that contract. A contract of May Sugar will be due for delivery on a certain date in May. If I **buy** May Sugar and do not complete the transaction by **selling** prior to that date I take delivery of tons of raw sugar (which is not a cataclysmic problem since it can be retendered for delivery next month).

Let's say I do buy a contract of May Sugar. On the commodity markets there is a seller for every buyer. I buy because I expect the price to increase and someone somewhere (probably an individual although it may be a company or institution) sells because they expect that the price of sugar will decrease. One of us will make money and the other will lose. We could also break even. The broker is smiling because he's made his money.

As far as the actual car loads of sugar are concerned I have absolutely no intention of taking delivery. I know from past experience and the number of other traders involved (about 32,000 in May sugar right now) that I can easily sell my contracts at any time I choose between now and May. It is as simple as phoning the broker and telling him to put in a sell order at a certain price level or date.

Which Option?

How do you decide on which option to trade? I look for several things when making this decision. First of all I look for high liquidity. I do not like to enter a market with open interest of less than 5,000 contracts and prefer those with at least 10,000 contracts outstanding. A thinly traded contract **may** be difficult to exit in the heat of sudden volatility and limit moves.

The second consideration is volatility. The nearby, or expiring, contract usually has larger price movements than the further contracts. This means that it offers better potential for profit but at the cost of greater risk. I usually opt for an option with a delivery date at least 2 months down the road. This allows time for a move to develop and keeps me out of the nervous markets of an expiring option.

Finally I look at the actual chart patterns. Chart makers often blow-up or enlarge the option with the greatest trading volume so that it is easier to keep the chart up dated. What I find with this "exploded" viewpoint is that it is difficult to visualize narrow trading channels and trends because the vertical distortion is so great. In such a case I tend to trade the option that meets the other considerations and also shows me a clear picture on the chart.

The Pits

If you have ever seen film footage of the action on the floor of the commodity exchanges in New York or Chicago you may wonder how on earth deals can ever be conducted amidst all the chaos and confusion. I wonder! But deals are made every minute of every trading day through shouting, hand signals, rude signs, and anything else that makes the point.

It is sheer bedlam but it works. My orders and trades are regularly filled on exchange floors thousands of miles away, in New York and Chicago, as the result of a phone call to my local broker.

Chapter 7

Longs and Shorts

Stock market players usually buy X number of shares of a particular company at the current price. Their positions are **long**; they make money only when the stock is increasing in value. It is relatively difficult to go **short** or sell a stock, although it is done every day.

On the commodity markets exactly half of all participants are long (have bought contracts) and half are short (have sold contracts). Sell orders are just as easy to execute on the commodity markets as are buy orders. This doubles your opportunities for entering money making trades because there are always markets which are declining, as well as rising.

Selling What You Don't Have

Selling what you don't yet own is a difficult concept for many people to grasp. If you are selling a contract it is an **obligation** to deliver the commodity by a certain date (expiry date for that particular option; eg: Dec Sugar, March Sugar, etc). It does **not** mean that you have to own the commodity when you are selling. All you are doing is **promising delivery by a certain date.**

When you sell you are counting on the price going down so that you can **buy at a lower price.** When the price goes down you buy and suddenly you **have** the commodity you promised to deliver earlier. In the end you sell high and buy low - which is what we are after. It is just in reverse order from buying first and then selling.

The contract is a promise to buy or sell the commodity in the future. As soon as you have bought and sold, in whatever order, you have completed the transaction. Any price difference between the level you buy at and sell at is **yours**; whether it is a profit or a loss.

Basis In Commodities

Basis is the difference between the cash price of a commodity and the nearest futures price for that commodity on the Exchange. Let us say that this is July 15 and the nearest contract option (in terms of expiry date) for Live Hogs on the Chicago Mercantile Exchange is due for delivery in August. In this example the cash price is 88 cents/lb. and the August contract is trading at 84 cents/lb. The cash market is at a **premium** to the futures price. There is sufficient demand for the actual commodity to keep the cash price higher than the price of Hogs for delivery in approximately a month. Basis is positive in this example.

Basis is easily arrived at by **subtracting the closing price of the nearest futures contract from the cash price.** If the result is a **positive** number the basis is positive. If the result is negative the basis is **negative**.

Basis is particularly important for those commodities where storage is an important factor in determining the price. This includes mainly the agricultural products such as meats, grains, food products, and cotton, etc. It is not an important consideration for precious metals or any of the financial markets.

Basis can be graphed just the same as a price history. Here is an example of a basis chart: (remember a **positive** value indicates a cash price **higher** than the futures price and a **negative** value indicates cash prices **lower** than the futures price).

Cash price determines the futures price. If the cash price is going up and basis is positive this give us a good indicator that the futures price should go up as well. If cash is going up and basis **switches** from negative to positive we have a particularly strong indicator that prices are moving into new ground.

Chapter 7

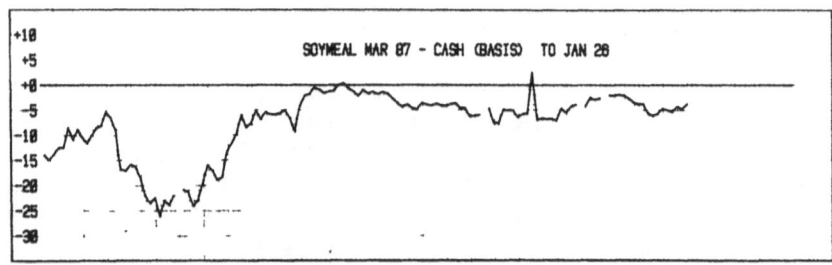

*Figure 7-1. An example of a **basis** chart for Soybean meal. Basis on this chart has remained negative for the complete time period, with the exception of a sharp thrust onto the positive side. This may be the first signal that basis is switching to the positive. If it did this would be one indicator to buy, or go long, the Soybean meal market.*

Seasonal Indicators

Agricultural commodities often follow seasonal patterns based on harvest season, slaughter times, weather cycles, etc. Seasonal patterns are available for most such commodities and can be another important factor in your trading strategy. I recommend that every serious commodity trader acquire a set of seasonal charts. One to look for is Seasonal Charts for Futures Traders: A Sourcebook by Courtney Smith, available through Investor Publications, Box 6, Cedar Falls, Iowa 50613.

Here are a few typical seasonal patterns:

110

Trading Comodities

Live Cattle Seasonal Pattern

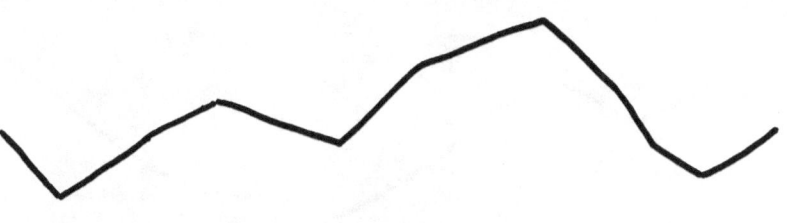

Live Hogs Seasonal Pattern

Corn Seasonal Pattern

Chapter 7

Wheat   Seasonal Pattern

Jan Feb Mar Apr May Jun Jul Aug Sep Oct Nov Dec

Soybeans   Seasonal Pattern

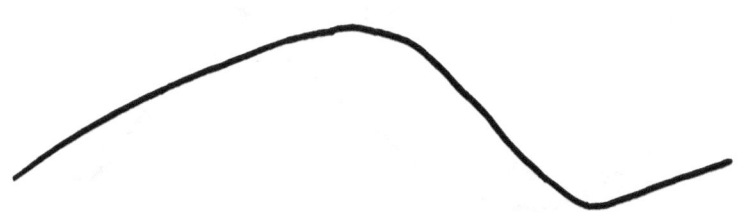

Jan Feb Mar Apr May Jun Jul Aug Sep Oct Nov Dec

Soybean Meal   Seasonal Pattern

Jan Feb Mar Apr May Jun Jul Aug Sep Oct Nov Dec

Soybean Oil   Seasonal Pattern

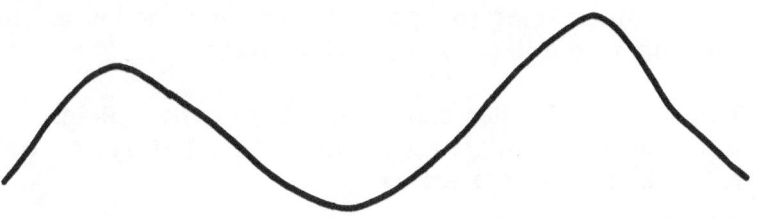

Jan Feb Mar Apr May Jun Jul Aug Sep Oct Nov Dec

If a commodity is following a typical seasonal pattern you can expect that it will continue to follow it in the near future unless something dramatic happens. This gives you another indicator in predicting the direction that the price will take. **A tradeable pattern** is still the first and foremost consideration but seasonal indicators should also be considered in helping you to plan your trades.

Limit Moves

In commodity trading some exchanges impose limits on the amount that the price is allowed to move in one trading period or day. If a commodity makes a **limit move**, particularly in a surging market, it must be watched very closely. This is usually the beginning of the end; the final blow-off in prices before there is a sudden correction. In this instance I will place my stop-loss just **within** the trading range so that if the market suddenly reverses I will be stopped out **before** it reaches the limit and all trading is halted.

The reasoning here is that the imposed limit often acts as a dam or barrier against the free flow of market sentiment. If the market goes down limit (or up limit) and trading is suddenly halted there is a tremendous amount of pressure built up when the market opens the following trading day. I have seen this pressure, on the Silver market for example, send the price plummeting 60% of previous gains in two days!

The one good thing about limit moves is that they are usually **in the direction** of the general trend. Since I always trade with the trend a limit move is almost always in my favour. Once such a move does occur, though, I watch the market **very closely** because it often becomes too volatile to trade reasonably.

Summary

1. Commodities offer the potential **to make a lot of money starting with a little** because of **leverage**.

2. Trading commodities can be extremely risky. Potential loss must be pre-calculated and planned for **before** the trade is entered. **Stop losses are essential**.

3. You are interested in making money on any **change in value** of a commodity, not in taking delivery.

4. A futures contract is a legally binding agreement.

5. It is **just as easy to sell short** as it is to go long. There are great opportunities in selling commodities **before** you buy them.

6. **Basis** is an important consideration in trading most agricultural commodities. When cash is higher than the futures price basis is **positive** and when cash is lower basis is **negative**.

7. **Seasonal indicators** form another important consideration for predicting possible price moves in agricultural markets.

8. **Limit moves** are a **warning** to watch the market very closely. Anything can happen (and usually does).

Chapter 8
Market Opportunities

A Line is a Line...

There are further opportunities to make money based on the ability to trade markets using account management skills and the basic strategies outlined in this book. In fact, my very first "investment", unintentional though it may have been, was along these lines.

Just after I finished University I made a trip to Europe, as all good North American students tended to do. I had read that the most acceptable currency for traveller's cheques in Europe, at that time, was the Swiss Franc. So I purchased $1,800 worth of Swiss Francs (this was in the spring of 1974) and headed off to experience the old country with a pack on my back.

I spent four months visiting the fjords of Norway, the Black Forest of Germany, the Swiss Alps, the Lake District in England ...until I grew weary and returned home. I still don't know how it happened but I had about $800 worth of Swiss Francs left when I arrived home. Surprise! The Swiss Franc had gone up appreciably against the Canadian dollar and my remaining $800 was now worth about $1,000. I had made $200 buying and selling Swiss Currency at the right time without even trying.

I wish it were that easy every time. But, based on this experience, I now realize that it is possible to trade commodities **without** having to buy and sell on the futures exchanges. Instead of trading contracts it is perfectly realistic to use the techniques outlined in this book to watch for trading opportunities and then

Chapter 8

trade by entering the **cash market**. This allows you to trade the commodity without entailing the risk normally associated with the leverage of a futures contract.

The returns associated with this type of investment are not as high as the potential returns involved in trading on the futures exchange. Neither are the risks! A person with very limited investment capital could begin in this way, gather valuable experience along the way and probably make enough to enter the stock or commodities market in the near future.

This could be a foot in the door for someone interested in starting slowly and building capital steadily with minimal risk.

Here are the steps involved in following this strategy:

1. Follow charts for the markets you are interested in, updating them daily from a financial newspaper

2. determine price levels and locations for buy or sell orders

3. instead of placing resting orders with a broker **prepare to buy or sell** the actual commodity when the predetermined price level is reached

4. follow the market with a **stop loss on paper** and close the trade at that price when it is hit.

Strong discipline is required in the application of these methods because, unless you can arrange it, your orders will not be carried out automatically. When a buy or sell signal is triggered you will probably have to complete the transaction yourself. The most importantly consideration is to keep track of the stop loss and **get out of the trade when it is hit.** No humming and hawing and rationalization - when the stop loss is hit it is time to exit the trade.

Market Opportunities

Trading Currencies

Instead of trading futures contracts on the exchanges we can purchase traveller's cheques in almost any currency at the larger banks. Follow the currencies by charting them yourself or acquiring charts from a financial publication or chart service and updating them regularly. I strongly recommend subscribing to a chart service even at this point in your trading career.

Using the information presented in this book watch for tradeable patterns and make preparations for purchasing the particular currency at the appropriate bank.

When a buy signal for Swiss Francs, for example, is triggered put your plan into action. Purchase a pre-determined amount of Swiss Franc traveller's cheques and put them away in a safety deposit box. Just let them sit there because **you never plan on using any of them.** You hold onto them until a sell signal (your stop loss) tells you to cash them in. There is a nominal transaction fee for this purchase but think of it as a very minimal commission. If the Swiss Franc does appreciate in value against the dollar, as you have predicted, your profits will more than cover the few dollars involved.

If you invest $1,000 in Swiss Francs and they appreciate 20% over 3 months your profit would be 20% or $200 (excluding any fees) in just 3 months. There is great potential for a high return in trading currencies because they tend to fluctuate frequently as global politics and economic trends in various nations change from month to month, and year to year.

Timing, as we have seen, is the important consideration. Anyone can go out and buy Swiss Francs because someone told them to or because they **hope** that the price will go up. **Few individuals** can make money buying and selling based solely on what they read in the newspapers or on tips from friends and advisors. They have no means of timing entry and exit into the market. By the time most investors read about an opportunity in the paper the largest part of the move has already occurred.

With this strategy **the market tells us when to take a position** and we do so based, not on mere hope, but on actual price signals.

Chapter 8

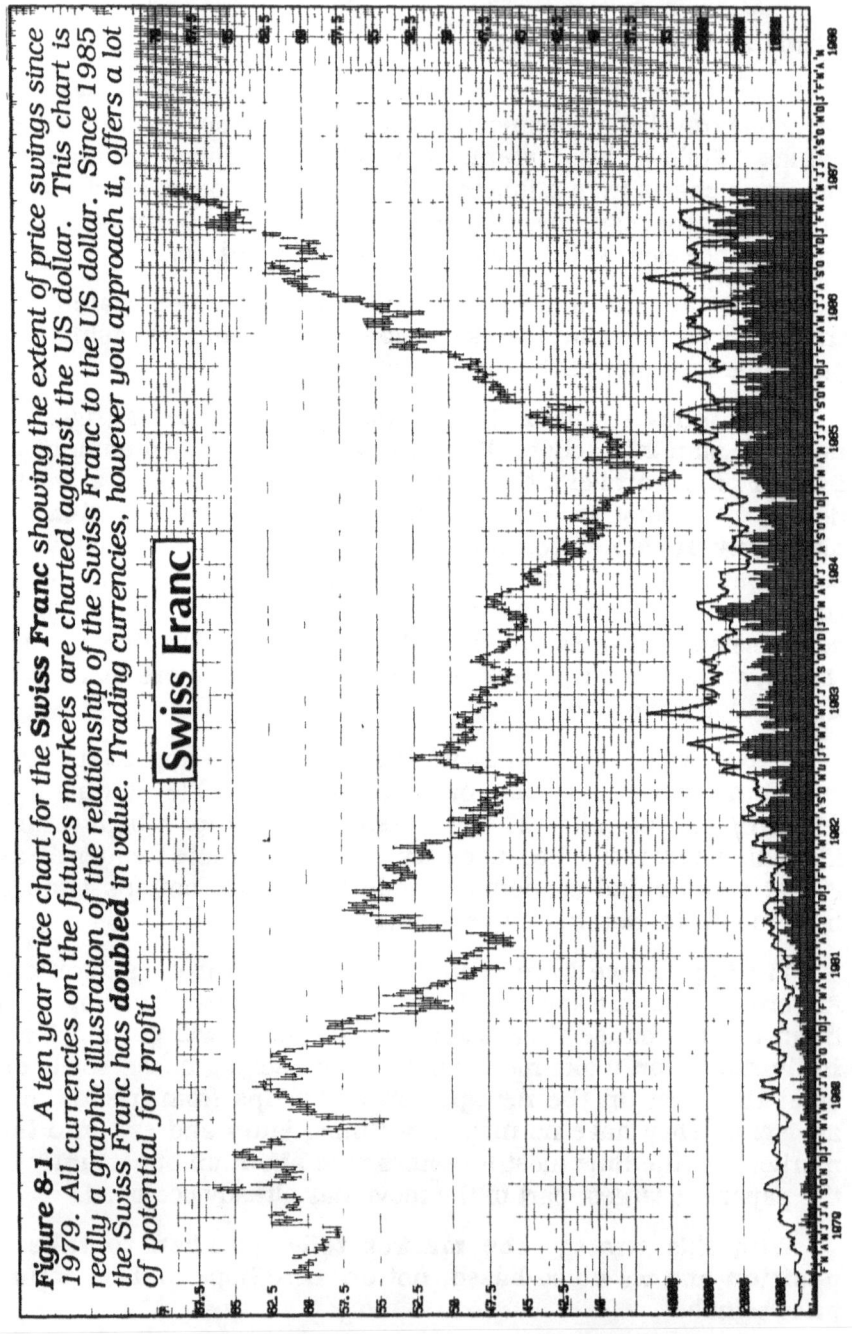

Figure 8-1. A ten year price chart for the **Swiss Franc** showing the extent of price swings since 1979. All currencies on the futures markets are charted against the US dollar. This chart is really a graphic illustration of the relationship of the Swiss Franc to the US dollar. Since 1985 the Swiss Franc has **doubled** in value. Trading currencies, however you approach it, offers a lot of potential for profit.

Market Opportunities

Precious Metals

The same techniques can be applied to trading in silver, gold, and, to a lesser extent, platinum. Follow the price charts for these precious metals and pre-negotiate purchase and storage or delivery details for the metal(s) you are interested in. You want to be able to purchase the metal very quickly; within a day or two of receiving a buy signal from the charts.

Take possession of the metal when your strategy indicates that you should buy. Put it away for safe keeping and don't touch it. Once again, you are not interested in using the metal or cashing it in too soon. Just hold onto the metal until a change in the up trend occurs, the market turns around, and your trailing stop loss is hit.

A variation on this strategy is to purchase **precious metal certificates** when the time is right. You don't actually take delivery but, as with a futures contract, you have the right to a certain amount of the metal which is stored for you in a secure location. The certificate guarantees you the right to that gold or silver, and to any change in value (up or down) until it is either cashed in or you decide to take delivery. A certificate is similar to holding a small futures contract, depending on the size of your purchase, without any leverage. You pay for the total amount of the commodity that you control.

Chapter 8

Mutual Funds

If you are interested in investing in a mutual fund why not get hold of a recent price chart and see exactly how the fund has been performing? It is relatively easy for fund managers to make fantastic claims about returns on a small amount invested 20 years ago but what you want to know is, "**which way is the fund headed right now?**".

Let's take the purely fictional case of a fund which has had spectacular results over the last 12 years but has recently peaked and has been headed steadily downhill for the last 5 months. The traditional approach to trading, based on price- level philosophy, would suggest that this fund **is now a good deal.**

Do you want to buy a mutual fund which has been in a down slide for the last 5 months? I don't. The salesperson will explain that mutual funds are a long term investment and that **this** is the time to buy because it **has to go back up** and if you buy now you will be one of the lucky smart ones to get in at the right time. Let someone else get lucky, I say. If I am interested in a particular fund it must be going my way - up. If it is going down I will wait for it to finish any downward motion, form a bottom, turn around, and then establish a definite up trend **before** I even consider buying.

My advice is to buy a mutual fund which is in an uptrend, update the chart at least weekly, and use a **trailing stop loss, on paper,** to take you out. When the fund turns around and falls through your stop loss level phone up the salesperson and tell him or her that you would like to cash in your investment immediately. They will try to talk you into hanging on but explain that you are watching closely for other opportunities which offer more potential. You can't afford to tie up your investment capital waiting for a fund to turn around. Let the person know that you will contact him or her when the time is right for the next purchase. The salesperson will soon see that you know what you are doing and leave the decisions up to you.

Most mutual funds can be traded in a manner similar to stocks. I would not trade those funds which charge front-end loading (a commission which is deducted from the initial payment) on a short term basis. It would become too expensive. Select those funds which charge a minimum commission or sales charge.

Market Opportunities

Summary

1. Use price charts to alert you of a potential trade in an actual cash market. Charts offer an unbeatable way of timing investments in currencies and precious metals.

2. Trade the metal or security by keeping track of prices on the chart and following the market with a trailing stop loss.

3. When the price level of the stop loss is violated **exit the trade**. Don't wait for the weather to change.

Appendix

Programmed Learning Charts

Programmed learning is another name for instructional methods, such as the use of flash cards, which allow you to experience logical sections of the material you are interested in learning about. It requires some involvement on the part of the subject and is, therefore, an active, rather than a passive, approach to learning.

In his book, HOW TO BE TWICE AS SMART, Scott Witt describes two benefits of programmed learning which are applicable to learning about almost anything, including trading stocks and commodities.

> First, repetition of facts in a **unique** way reinforces your memory, and

> Second, active recall causes you to **actively** think about the material.

Remember the days back at school when you sat with a deadpan expression on your face as the teacher tried her best to fill your head with English grammar. Do you remember the foggy, heavy feeling as you sat endured another half hour just waiting for the noon hour bell to ring. Was it difficult to stay awake? Especially when the sun broke through the high windows and pooled at your feet, and the flies buzzed from one sunny spot to the next? Remember the smell of chalk...

This is the feeling of **passive** learning.

There are probably many reasons that most of us never did learn much grammar. I would guess that the biggest one was **lack of motivation**. Not many of us were really all that interested in grammar in grades six and seven. I certainly weren't. Another is that we usually absorbed the information, used it for a few quick exercises, and then promptly filed it away, never to actively recall it again.

Trading stocks and commodities is another matter. You are obviously interested or you wouldn't have made it this far in the book and, hopefully, you will be using this material frequently over the next few days, months, and years.

In order to give you a head start on application of the material we have covered in this book I have prepared three interactive programmed learning exercises for you to practice your charting, trading, and account management skills. I have rolled four to six weeks of **real** trading experience into the following few pages.

The programmed learning appendix is broken into three separate sections:

    I.   The Instructions and Price Data Table.
           -price data and instructions for all three markets

    II.   The Working price charts
           -selected patterns from historic price charts

    III. The Final Results charts
           -the same historic price charts but a few months older so you can see how your chart should look

I. Instructions

You will find price charts on the following pages for three actual markets from the last few years. These are authentic price records and you will be able to trade them exactly as if they were happening right now.

Go to the Price Data Table and you will see daily price ranges for each market (Market A, B, and C) beginning on the day that the working price chart ends. Each daily quote includes the high and low for that day. I have scrambled the daily quotes to maintain the element of surprise found in real life.

To find the prices for Market A start at A-1 and look down the column three spaces for A-2, three more spaces for A-3, three more for A-4... etc. Follow Market B and C the same way. Start at B-1 and go down three spaces to B-2, etc. I suggest using a piece of paper to mask the rest of the page as you go down so you have no hint of prices to come.

Draw trendlines, locate resting buy or sell orders and the initial stop loss, and mark them on the chart. Now, take a piece of graph paper for each market and write the appropriate prices along the right hand margin and transfer the stop orders from the price chart. Continue charting where the price charts in the book leave off. If your order is hit consider yourself in the market!

Remember, this is supposed to duplicate actual trading that you would be doing on these markets. For your purposes these markets are happening right now so here is your opportunity to trade as if you had the chance to make real money on them, today.

All three of these markets are commodity markets so you should calculate the change in value for each cent or dollar move, depending on the market, based on the price scale and the "value of move = $XX" figure at the top of the chart.

I would use the following approach to trade each market:

- draw trendlines and identify points of resistance and support

- predict the direction of the move based on this technical information (in real life you would also have the benefit of fundamental information)

- determine price levels and locations for resting orders and initial stop losses and draw them in

- follow the market with a trailing stop once your order is "filled"

- trade it exactly as if real cash was involved

On the following page you will find the Price Data Table.

Have fun trading.

Price Data Table

A-1	448-434	B-18	660-640
B-1	765-752	C-18	72.15-71.60
C-1	75.10-75.00	A-19	476-470
A-2	443-436	B-19	660-645
B-2	745-728	C-19	71.70-71.20
C-2	74.90-74.70	A-20	484-478
A-3	442-436	B-20	670-640
B-3	770-745	C-20	71.45-71.20
C-3	74.75-74.55	A-21	500-490
A-4	439-436	B-21	650-638
B-4	780-750	C-21	71.30-71.05
C-4	74.70-74.55	A-22	523-498
A-5	445-437	B-22	655-635
B-5	775-760	C-22	71.50-71.10
C-5	74.60-74.45	A-23	548-534
A-6	447-442	B-23	660-630
B-6	775-760	C-23	71.35-70.80
C-6	74.60-74.50	A-24	550-528
A-7	444-442	B-24	670-645
B-7	758-748	C-24	71.25-70.95
C-7	74.40-74.30	A-25	563-525
A-8	456-441	B-25	650-640
B-8	750-722	C-25	71.80-71.35
C-8	74.35-74.20	A-26	548-528
A-9	453-448	B-26	650-635
B-9	730-710	C-26	71.75-71.15
C-9	74.30-74.20	A-27	550-538
A-10	452-446	B-27	650-630
B-10	730-720	C-27	71.90-71.50
C-10	74.40-74.20	A-28	542-530
A-11	448-436	B-28	635-620
B-11	745-730	C-28	71.70-71.35
C-11	73.95-73.80	A-29	542-530
A-12	450-442	B-29	640-620
B-12	740-710	C-29	71.90-71.55
C-12	73.70-73.70	A-30	560-540
A-13	450-446	B-30	625-615
B-13	710-695	C-30	72.20-71.80
C-13	73.00-72.70	A-31	583-552

Price Data Table

A-14	455-448	B-31	625-615
B-14	685-665	C-31	72.65-72.25
C-14	72.20-71.35	A-32	594-567
A-15	453-450	B-32	630-620
B-15	680-660	C-32	72.60-72.25
C-15	71.55-70.55	A-33	590-570
A-16	453-450	B-33	630-620
B-16	700-680	C-33	72.80-72.50
C-16	71.65-70.65	A-34	598-582
A-17	470-458	B-34	655-640
B-17	680-660	C-34	72.75-72.25
C-17	72.25-71.50	A-35	596-576
A-18	473-462	B-35	650-640

C-35	72.25-71.85
A-36	616-598
A-37	632-618
A-38	652-640
A-39	664-644
A-40	676-635
A-41	682-670
A-42	670-652
A-43	640-628
A-44	645-590
A-45	578-540
A-46	596-563

Programmed Learning Charts
Section II

Working Price Charts

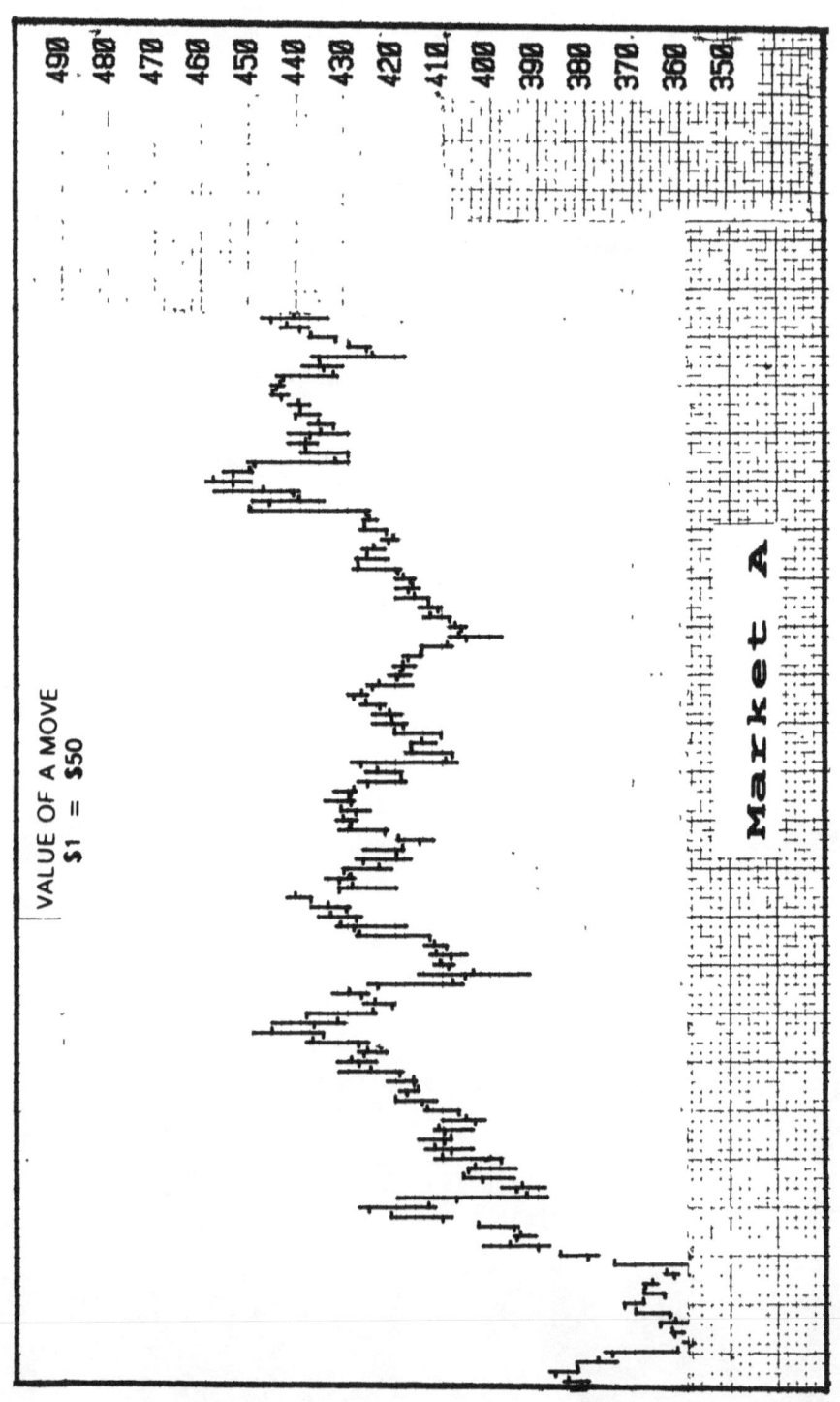

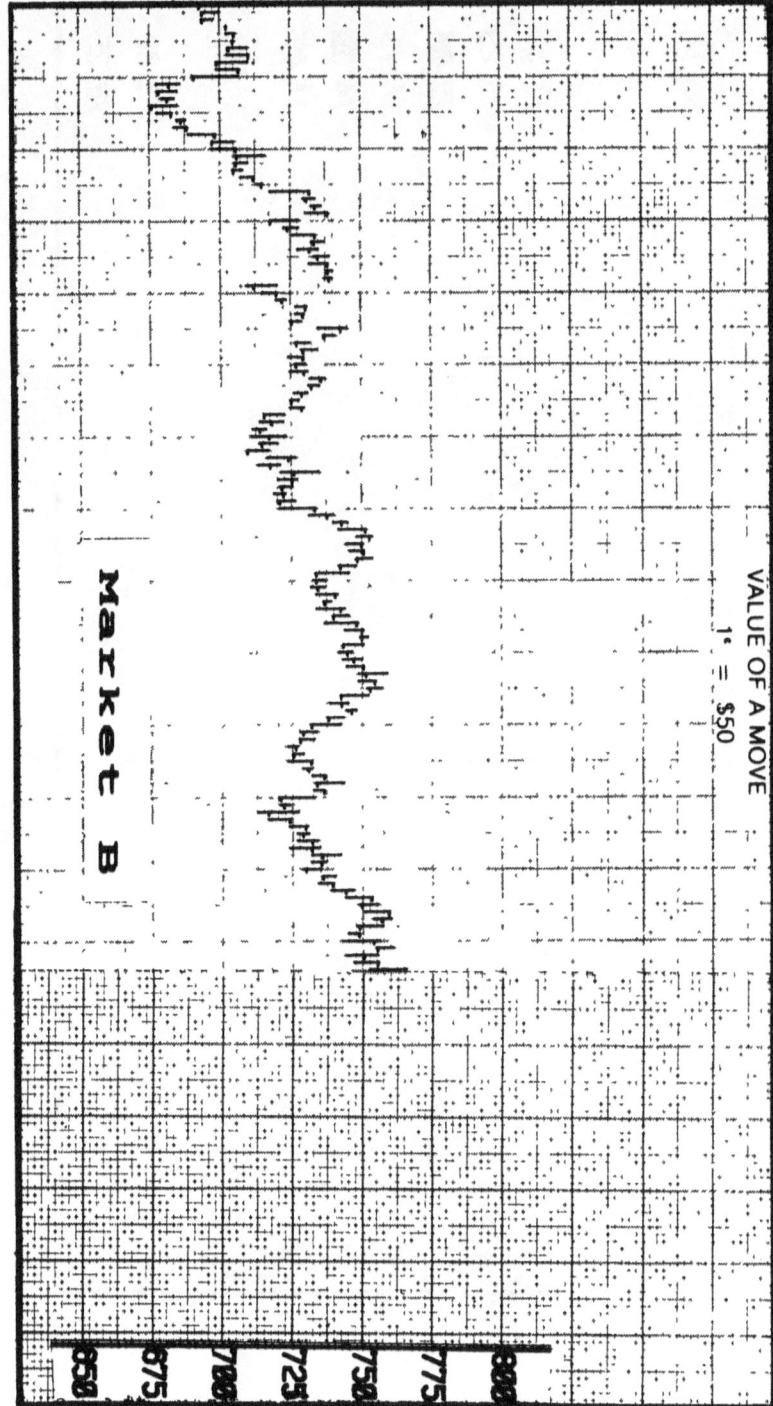

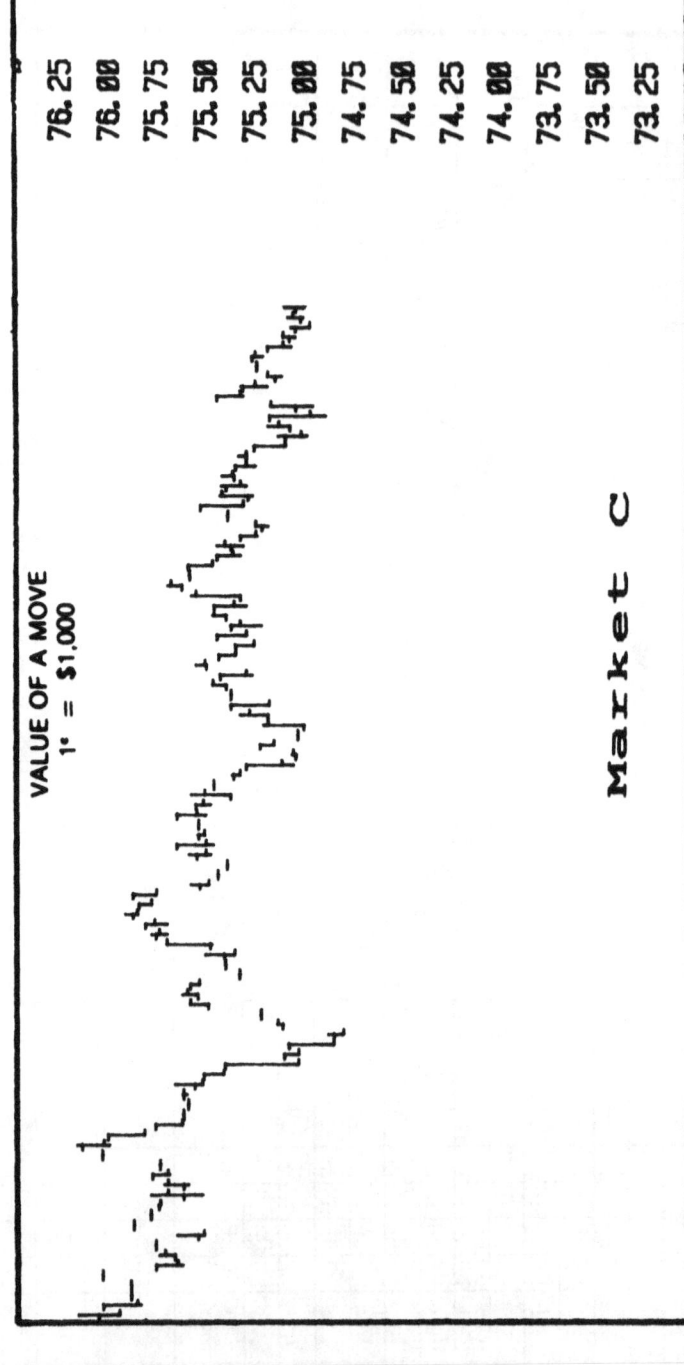

Programmed Learning
Section III

Final Results Charts

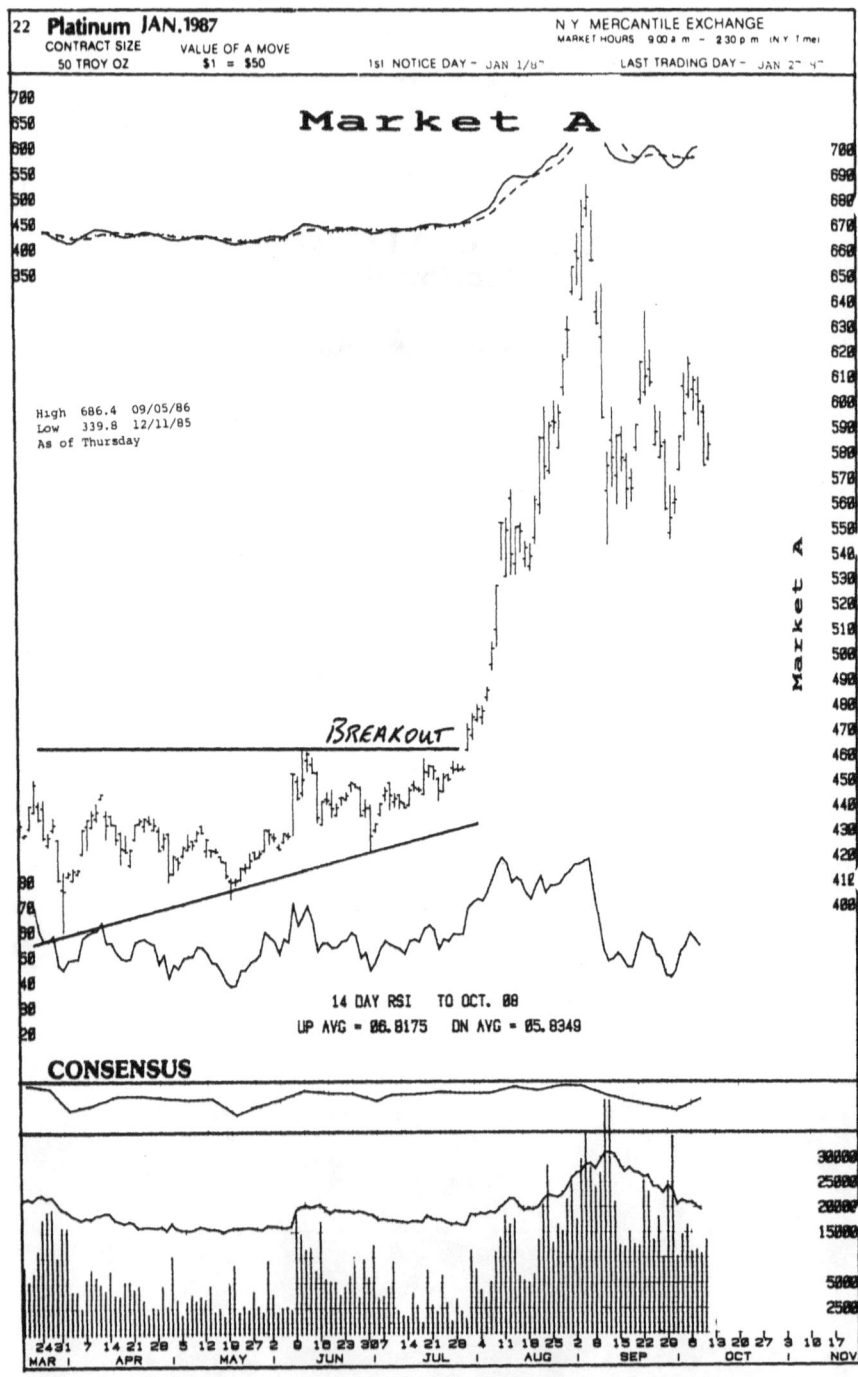

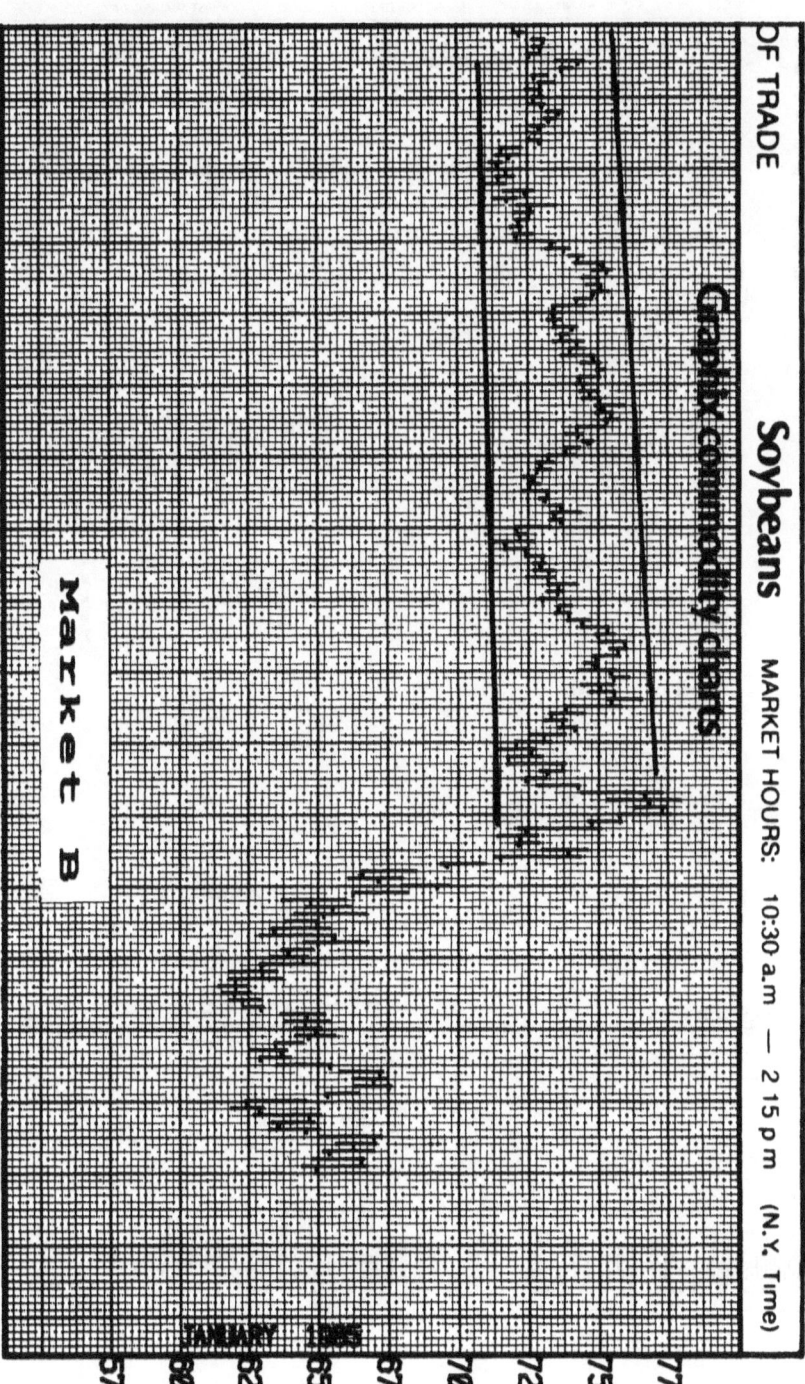

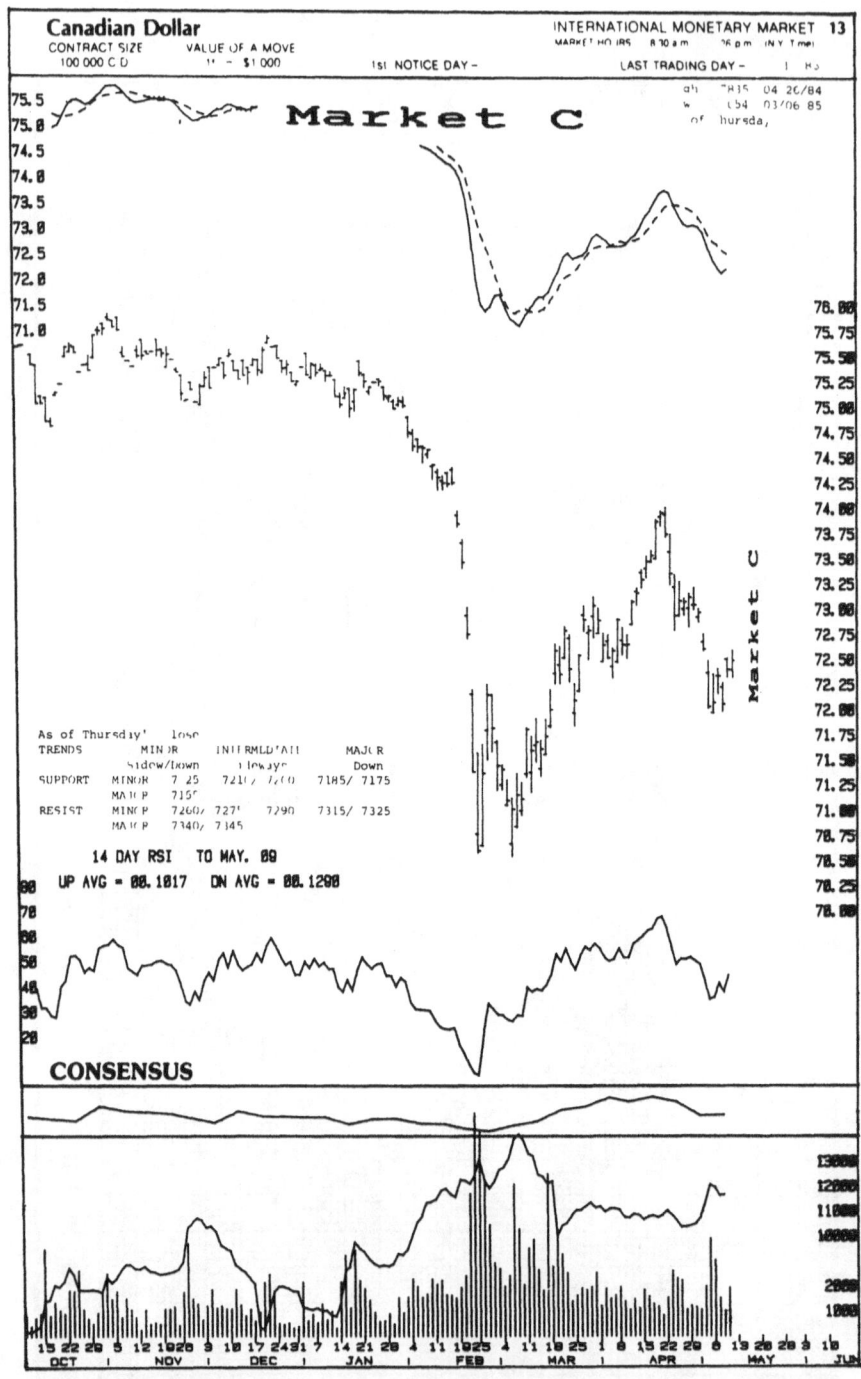

Bibliography

Commodity Trading Manual, Bruce Gould, Bruce Gould Publications, Box 16, Seattle, Wash. 98111. The best in-depth treatment of trading commodities that I have read. This book is required reading if you are serious about commodities.

How to Be Twice as Smart, Scott Witt, Parker Publishing Co. Inc, New York, ISBN 0-13-402339-0. All about more effective learning techniques, active listening skills, and communication skills. Excellent reading.

How to Make Money in Commodities, Bruce Gould, Bruce Gould Publications, Box 16, Seattle, Wash. 98111. This is the best primer on trading commodities that I have run across.

Imagineering: How to Profit from Your Creative Powers, Michael LeBoeuf, McGraw Hill Book Company, ISBN 0-07-036954-2. An excellent book on goals and creativity.

Take The Guessing Out of Investing, Sydney Tremayne, 1987, Prentice-Hall, ISBN 0-13-882630-7. A good primer of technical trading techniques for the stock market.

The Magic of Thinking Big, David Schwartz, 1959, Prentice-Hall, Inc., ISBN 0-346-12292-9. Great motivation for setting your sights high and then going for it.

The Book of Books on Wall Street Speculation, "Don Guyon", 1965, Fraser Publishing Company, Box 494, Burlington, Vermont 05402, ISBN 0-87034-013-1. First published in 1917, this tiny book rings as true today as it did back then. Shows how little things really change once you learn how to make money on the markets.

The Omega Strategy: How You Can Retire Rich by 1986, William Montapert, 1982, Capra Press, Santa Barbara, California, ISBN 0-88496-187-7. A good overview of world economics and strategies for profiting from changing situations.

Wishcraft: How to Get What You Really Want, Barbara Sher, 1979, Ballantine Books, New York, ISBN 345-34089-2. This is an excellent book on establishing concrete goals, plotting a strategy for achieving them, and then doing it.

You Can Have It All: The Art of Winning the Money Game and Living a Life of Joy, Arnold Patent, 1987, Money Mastery Publishing, ISBN 0-9613663-1-1. A exciting approach to making money and the notion of natural abundance in life.

Glossary of Trading Terms

Actuals: The physical or cash commodity, as distinguished from a futures contract.

Appreciation: An increase in value.

Arbitrage: A buying and selling technique used to take advantage of price differences between two or more futures contracts or a stock traded on different markets.

Asset Value: The monetary value of holdings, sometimes expressed as asset value per share by dividing the total asset figure by the number of shares outstanding.

Average or Index: Indicators of broad market performance based on a selected group of stocks or commodities.

Basis Point: 1/100th of a percentage point, used to indicate small moves in interest rates or currencies.

Basis Grade: The grade of a commodity used as the standard for the contract.

Basis: The difference between the spot or cash price of a commodity and the futures price of the same commodity. Basis is usually calculated to the nearby option.

Bear Market: A market in which prices are declining.

Bear: One who expects a decline in prices.

Bearish: When conditions suggest a lower price a bearish situation is said to exist. The opposite of bullish.

Bid: An offer to buy a specific quantity of a stock or commodity at a stated price.

Blue Chip: Companies with a history of good management, profitable growth and uninterrupted dividend payments.

Book Value: The value of net assets as shown on a company's balance sheet.

Break: A rapid or sharp decline in prices.

Breakup Value: The value of a comapany's assets if they are sold as separate divisions.

Broker: A person paid a fee or commission for executing buy or sell orders for a customer.

Bull Market: A market in which prices are rising.

Bull: One who expects an advance in prices.

Bullion: Gold in bars or ingots assaying at least .995 fine.

Bullish: When conditions suggest a higher price a bullish situation is said to exist. The opposite of bearish.

Buy on Opening: To buy at the beginning of a trading session within the opening price range.

Buy On Close: to buy at the end of the trading session with the closing price range.

Call Option: The right to buy an asset for a specified price within a specified period of time. A price, or premium, is usually paid for the option.

Cash Price: the price in the marketplace for actual cash or spot commodities to be delivered via customary market channels.

Cash Market: Market for immediate delivery of and payment for commodities.

Cash Commodity: The physical or actual commodity as distinguished from the futures contract.

CFO: Cancel former order.

Charting: The use of graphs and charts in the technical analysis of stock and futures markets to plot trends, price patterns, moving averages, volume and open interest.

Churning: Excessive trading which permits the broker to derive a profit from commissions without keeping the best interests of the client in mind.

Close, The: The period at the end of the trading session officially designated by the exchange during which all transactions are considered to be made "at the close".

Closing Price: The price recorded in trading that takes place in the final moments of a day's trade officially designated as the "close".

Commission: The charge made by a brokerage house for buying and selling commodities or stocks.

Commitment or Open Interest: The number of contracts in existence at any period of time which have not as yet been satisfied by an offsetting sale or purchase.

Common Share: A class of stock that represents ownership or equity in a company. Such shares may be voting or non-voting.

Congestion: A term used in technical analysis for a period of limited price fluctuations which appears as a quiet market trending sideways.

Contract Month: The month in which delivery is to be made in accordance with a futures contract.

Contract Grades: Those grades of a commodity which have been officially approved by an exchange for settlement of a futures contract.

Contract: A term of reference describing a unit of trading for a commodity. A contract specifies the quantity, quality, delivery date, and location.

Convertible preferred share: Securities that can be converted into a company's common stock at a specified rate of exchange.

Current Delivery: The futures contract which matures for delivery in the current month.

Day Trading: Entering and exiting the same futures market position within the same day.

Day Order: An order that expires automatically at the end of each day's trading session.

Delivery Month: the specified month within which a futures contract matures and can be settled by delivery.

Delivery: The tender and receipt of the actual commodity in the settlement of a futures contract.

Depository or Warehouse Receipt: A document issued by a bank, warehouse, or other depository indicating ownership of a stored commodity.

Derivative Instruments: Options on stocks and stock indices that reflect the underlying value of common stocks and are traded by speculators.

Discount: The price difference between futures of different delivery months.

Dividend: A portion of profit paid to shareholders to provide a return on investment. May be paid in cash or stock. May be declared quarterly or for other time periods.

Equity: The net interest of an owner or shareholder.

Exchange: A place or system through which securities and futures contracts or other instruments can be traded.

First Notice Day: The first day on which notices of intention to deliver actual commodities can be received.

Float, Stock: Shares of a company that are not owned by controlling shareholders and are available for trading.

Front-end Load: Commissions or sales charges deducted from initial payments into a mutual fund.

Fundamental Analysis: Study of basic, underlying factors which affect the supply and demand of a stock or commodity.

Futures: A term used to designate the standardized contracts covering the sale of commodities for future delivery on a commodity exchange.

Futures Market: A market which is set up specifically for hedgers to transfer their risk to speculators who willingly take on the risk in exchange for the potential to profit.

Hedging: A position taken in a commodity or securities market opposite to a position held in the cash market, or another security, to minimize the risk of financial loss from an adverse price change.

Initial Margin: Customer's funds put up as security for a guarantee of contract fulfillment at the time a futures market position is established.

Insider: A senior company official, significant shareholder, or anyone who might have confidential information about a company's financial or corporate affairs.

Last Trading Day: Day on which trading ceases for the current delivery month on a commodity exchange.

Leverage: Buying or selling the right to a stock or commodity on margin for a small percentage of the actual value.

Limit Move: A price that has advanced or declined the permissible limit in one trading session.

Limit (Up or Down): the maximum price movement from the previous day's closing price permitted by an exchange.

Limit Order: An order in which the customer sets a limit on price or other conditions, such as time of an order, as contrasted with a market order which should be filled as soon as possible.

Liquid Assets: Cash or other assets that can be readily converted to cash.

Liquid Market: A market which is easy to enter or exit with minimal price change.

Listed Stock: Shares of a company that are listed for trading on a stock exchange.

Long: One who has bought an interest in a stock or futures contract.

M.I.T. Order: (Market If Touched) An order that becomes a market order when a particular price is reached.

Margin Call: A request from a brokerage firm to a customer to bring margin deposits up to minimum required levels.

Margin: The amount of money or collateral deposited by a client with his broker for the purpose of insuring the broker against a loss on an open position. Initial margin is the amount when the position is opened and maintenance margin is a sum which must be maintained on deposit at all times.

Market Order: An order to buy or sell at whatever price is obtainable at the time it is entered on the floor of the exchange, or pit.

Minority Shareholders: Those who do not have a controlling or significant share ownership in a company.

Money Market: The market on which short-term debt securities are traded.

Mutual Fund: A professionally managed pool of money raised from many participants and invested in securities. Value of each unit is determined by the total worth of the investments divided by the number of units outstanding.

Open Order (also G.T.C. Order):Good Til Cancelled. An open order remains in force until the customer explicitly cancels it or, in the case of the futures market, the contract expires.

Option: An agreement to buy or sell an asset at an agreed price within a specified time. A price, or premium, is usually paid for an option.

Paper Profit: Profit realized only on paper without actually entering into the transaction.

Paper Trading: Carrying out all aspects of an investment program except for entering the transactions with actual cash.

Portfolio: A range of investments maintained in accordance with investment goals and risk considerations.

Preferred Share: A class of stock having privileges attached to it, usually a claim on dividends before the common stock.

Price/Earnings Ratio: The price of a stock divided by its annual share profit.

Proxy: A formal document that gives an absent shareholder's vote to someone else at a company meeting.

Pyramiding: The use of profits on previous positions as margin to increase the size of the position.

Range: The difference between the high and low price during a given period.

Resting Order: An order to buy or sell above or below the present market price.

Retained Earnings: A company's net accumulation of profit after deducting dividends paid out.

Return on Capital: Annual profit measured as percentage return on the amount of both debt and equity capital invested in the business.

Return on Assets: Annual profit measured as percentage return on value of a company's assets.

Short: One who has sold an interest in a security or commodity.

Speculator: An individual who does not hedge, but who trades with the objective of achieving profits through the successful anticipation of price movements.

Stock Split: The division of shares, say two for one, to make more stock available for trading and to attract investors who might buy in at a lower price.

Stop Order: An order that becomes a market order when a particular price level is reached. A sell stop is below the market and a buy stop is placed above.

Stop-loss Order: A stop order used to exit a position in order to prevent large losses or "lock in" profits.

Technical Analysis: Using charts and graphs to analyze future trends, patterns of price change, moving averages, open interest and volume.

Trend: The general direction, either upward, downward or sideways, in which prices are moving.

Volume: The number of securities or futures contracts traded during a specified period of time.

Warrant: A security conferring the right to buy the shares of a company at a specified price within a specified period.

INDEX

80/20 Rule	20	Crude oil	58
		Currencies	117

A

Acceptable loss	86
Agricultural commodities	110
Automatic	
entry	75
exit	75
protection	90

D

Deadlines	20
Demand	47
Depression	10
Direction	73
Discipline	55, 116
Down-trend	64

B

Bad luck	76
Bargains	41
Basis commodities	109
Beliefs	43
Breaking even	42
Breakout	44, 61, 70
signal	34
strategy	15, 53
Broker	101
Business	
cycle	68
decisions	48
plan	14

E

Elliot Wave Theory	68
Emotion	76, 91
Entry	75
Equity	42
Established	44
range	51, 70
trend	30
Exit	65, 75
Experience	10, 13

C

Canadian Dollar	28
Cash market	116
Cash price commodities	109
Change in Value	104
Channels	55
Charting	28
Charts weekly	28
Choice stocks	97
Coffee	40, 59
Commissions	11
Commodity	
charts	13
labels	106
Congestion	
pattern	60
phase	32
Course correction	63

F

Fears	43
Financial goals	14
Fortune	15
Fragmentation goals	19
Fundamental factors	7, 42, 98
Futures contract	28
delivery	106
expiry	106
size	105
value of a move	105

G

Gamble	6
Game plan	10
Goal	63
Goals	17
Gold	43
Granduc Mines Limited	57

H

Hedge	103
Hemlo Gold Mines	56
Hopes	43
Hot tips	76

I

Inflation	10
Inside information	9
Investment Criteria	1

K

Knowledge	12

L

Level of risk	5
Leverage	3, 103, 116
Limit move	95, 113
Limited Risk	4
Line	23
Liquidity	28
Long	54, 108
Losses	42
Luck	5

M

Managed accounts	11
Margin	4
Market Opportunities	115
Market Psychology	43
Marketplace	32
Mass psychology	63
Maximizing Profit	94
McConnell - Peel Resources	62
Momentum	15, 65
Money making skill	54
Mortgage	4
Motivation	20
Movement traders	41
Mutual Funds	120

N

Narrow trading range	32
New York Commodity Exchange	60

O

Odds	53
Open interest	107
Over-valued	40
Overtrade	55
Overtrading	11

P

Palladium	80
Paper loss	42
Paper profits	10
Paper trading	13, 105
Patterns	37, 47
chart	23
Percentage Profit	69
Perceptions	43
Placement - stop loss	92
Plan, business	6
Position traders	40
Potential for Growth	2
for profit	14, 31
Pre-calculate Loss	86
Precious metal certificates	119
Precious Metals	119
Preparation	76
Price chart	24, 25, 28
Price histories	23
Price pattern	47, 106
Price Quotes	28
Price range	26
Priorities	20
Production cost	43
Psychological barrier	89
Psychology of marketplace	37, 53
Pyramiding	84

R

Real estate market	24
Resistance	31, 36, 52
Resting buy order	78, 81
Resting order	78
Returns	116
Reversal Points	87
Risk	14, 116
Rules of Trading	74, 77

S

Scale-in strategy	15, 82
Seasonal Indicators	110
Seasonal patterns	110, 112, 113
Seasonal tendencies	7
Selling	108
Selling short	53
Sequential waves	15, 44, 63, 65
Set of rules	74
Shares	9
Short	53, 108
Sideways channel	32, 54, 59
Signals	37
Silver	58, 60
Speculators	103
Stability	32, 70
Stock charts	13, 25, 99
Stocks	14
Stop loss	85
placement	65, 92
Strategies	39
price	40
price level	40
momentum	40
Success Strategy	7
Successive highs	31
lows	30
Sugar	26, 104
Supply and demand	32, 47
Support	30, 36
Surging market	59
stop losses	94
Swiss Franc	118

T

Technical	42
Technical factors	87
Technical patterns	7, 78
Timeframe	5
Timing	43, 79
Tradeable pattern	44, 50, 61, 113
favourite	54
Trading Commodities	103
Trading Intelligently	45
Trading Stocks	97
strategy	100
Trading strategy	7
Trailing stop loss	8, 91, 93
Treasury Bills	104
Trend	7, 37
definition	38
duration	32
long term	34
medium term	33
short term	33
Trending market	69
Trendline	30 - 52
strength	38, 51
Trends	30

U

Under-valued	40
Underpriced	40
Up-trend	64

V

Visualization	18
Volatility	107

W

Warrants	9
Wave Theories	68
Wealth	15, 24

www.ingramcontent.com/pod-product-compliance
Lightning Source LLC
Chambersburg PA
CBHW030745180526
45163CB00003B/923